1 HABIT™ FOR WOMEN ACTION TAKERS

LIFE CHANGING HABITS FROM THE HAPPIEST ACHIEVING WOMEN ON THE PLANET

CREATED AND COMPILED BY STEVEN SAMBLIS

CO-AUTHOR LYNDA SUNSHINE WEST

1 Habit™ For Women Action Takers

By Steven Samblis and many other Happy Achievers.

Published by Envision Media Press, a division of Envision Media Partners, Inc.

The publishers gratefully acknowledge the individuals that contributed to this book.

To my Daughters Lindsay and Kaitlyn

TABLE OF CONTENTS

FORWARD

Welcome to the second book in the 1 Habit series.

When I created the 1st book (1 Habit), I had no idea the impact it would have on people. Both readers and contributors turned it from a simple book into a movement.

As I sit here now and write this forward, we have 24 more books to follow this one. We will publish one book a month for the next 24 months. Each book will follow the 1 Habit formula, and the exciting part is each book has a Co-Author.

These Co-Authors are experts in various walks of life, each with huge followings. We will use the 1 Habit formula to tap into Habits for areas like Music, Entrepreneurship, Creativity, Athletics, and many more.

I am very excited that you now own this incredible book built by Women Action Takers. When my Co-Author, Lynda Sunshine West, came to me with the idea of doing a 1 Habit Book For Women Action Takers, my responses was an immediate yes.

Our initial plan was to do a webinar with a few hundred potential contributors and publish the book about a month later.

As the webinar was in process, I had an inspiration. These women we were talking to where all "Action Takers." They made things happen. They ran big companies. Some started big companies. All of them took charge of their lives and created the success they knew they wanted. So, why not challenge them to do the impossible (in most people's eyes)

It was on November 18th. Next week would be Thanksgiving in the US. Let's take action and have this book publish by the week of Thanksgiving. Now, keep in mind the first book took nine months to bring all the contributors together, layout, edit, artwork, and everything else to bring it to market. I was asking these incredible women to show who they were. It would take an astonishing group of people to come together and take a book from concept to market in what amounted to be just 12 days.

Everyone agreed that they would up for the challenge. My Co-Author and I created a system for submissions, which would streamline the process. We brought on more people to handle editing and design, and we hit the start button.

Within the first 24 hours, we had 1/4 of the submissions in. By day two we had another 1/4. As each submission came is, we edited them, laid them out, and sent proofs back to the contributors to take another pass at and return.

Seven days after that initial webinar, we were doing the final pass of edits to the final draft of the book. We finished those within 18 hours.

As I sit here right now, I am writing the final words to be placed into this book. When I finish, we will send this to our distributors, and the book will be available for people to purchase in 3 days.

If anybody asks me why they should listen to the women in this book and follow their Habit, my answer is simple. I was a witness and a participant in seeing them do the impossible. These women came together, walking their talk, and created a book of Habits in 8 days.

The most important part for you, dear reader, is the fact that if you take one of these Habits and make it a part of you, it may change your life forever. Take five and instill them inside of yourself, you may change the world.

Steven Samblis

Creator of 1 Habit™

THE CREATION OF THE 1 HABIT™ MOVEMENT

 My name is Steven Samblis, and it is my honor to present to you 1 Habit For Women Action Takers™. I hope this book will have a profound effect on your life. For you to get the most out of this book, I feel it is essential that I share with you how the 1 Habit™ Movement was created, and more importantly, why it was created. After, we will show you how to use the book to reach your maximum potential.

I say the following with absolute certainty. If you walk away and have taken ownership of just one of the habits in this book, It will have a profound effect on your life. I know this because when I learned the power of habits and instilled the first one into who I was, my life changed forever. I know the same can happen to you, and here is where it gets exciting. Add on another habit and another after that, and you will find your life taking off on automatic pilot to the greatness that you were born to achieve.

The Beginning

From the time I was a young man, brand new to the business, I knew the way to be successful in my chosen field was to find successful people that came before me and do the things that they did. I was a stockbroker at the time. I would find the most successful stockbrokers in the business and study what they did every day. I then began to do the same things. I would start my day at the same time. I went to lunch at the same time. I ate dinner at the same time. I went home at the same time. I made calls when they where making calls and studied the market when they did. After the end of doing this for six months, I was mentally and physically fried. Something was missing.

One of my heroes at this point in my life was a stockbroker named Al Glover. Al worked with me at a Stock Brokerage firm in Cocoa Beach, Florida. It was the early 80's, and Cocoa Beach was a town where a charming house cost $50,000.00. Al was taking down a few million a year in commissions in this sleepy little beach little town.

Al's office was right across from mine, so I every once in a while I would pop in his doorway and ask him how he became so successful, hoping to find the key. On one particular day, Al told me to sit down, watch, and listen.

As he stood behind his desk, he picked up the phone and called a client, whom he later me was a huge client but somewhat challenging to deal with. She always over-analyzed his recommendations, and by the time she was ready to pull the trigger, it was too late. "Mrs. Rooney, we have a terrific tax free bond yielding 8%, and I thought you would be interested." Al delivered the words, sat down, and shut up. It felt like an eternity went by as he sat silently on the phone, waiting for her response. "I have worked with you for many years, and during that time, you have missed out on incredible opportunities, which would have made you a great deal of money. This will be one of those. You have the money sitting in your Money Market, making a few points taxable. If you do not take this position, I am not doing my job and will no longer be able to be your Financial Advisor. I will pass your account on to somebody else." Al then stopped talking and waited. Another eternity went by until Al said. "Great, we will buy $200,000.00. I will place the order for you in the morning. Great decision. Talk to you soon."

I looked at Al stunned. "You were willing to throw away one of your biggest clients if she had said no?" Al went on to tell me, every day he looked at his book of 2000 clients and picked the five most difficult, called them and gave them one shot to turn around the relationship or he would dump them as clients. Al had instilled in himself a habit of looking at his business every day at 6 pm and making calls to remove things in it that deterred from his happiness. He said every day; this one habit gave him a tremendous sense of peace. Same time every day. Most of the clients just needed that nudge to understanding what a good position they were in having him manage their money, and their attitudes and how they worked together became dramatically better. Those phone calls each day at 6 pm, that single Habit had a profound effect on Al's business and happiness.

As I left Al's office, I was inspired. I was motivated and worked hard, but motivation is just the thing that gets you started. It is habits like Al's 6 pm calls that keep you going and drive you down the pathway to success. Motivation is what gets you started, but it is your Habits that keep you going.

Habits, once a part of you, are automatic. They do not require mental pushing and do not drain you of energy. They guide you along the right path.

I went to my office, sat on my chair, and bounced up and went right back to Al's office. "Al, this is an amazing habit, the 6 pm calls. However, I do not have 2000 clients. What one habit could I make part of me that would get me to that 2000 client number?" Al took a moment and told me in a very matter of fact way. "Every night before you go home. Map out your next day. If you have clients or prospects you will want to call tomorrow, make a list before you go home. If you have a trade ticket that you need to place in the morning, write it out before. Set yourself up for success every day by preparing the night before." Wow. He was so right! That Habit sets the tone for my future success. I eventually instilled other habits now that I have learned how it all works. This, in turn, leads to me to my goal of having over 2000 clients in the next five years. From that moment on, I lived my life with the understanding, "Motivation is what gets you started, but it is your habits that keep you going."

Fast forward to 2 years ago. I was filming interviews at the weekend Entrepreneurship Conference for Envision TV. This incredible gathering was attended by some of the highest achievers on the planet. As we prepared to roll the interviews, a thought of my friend Al came to me. "Habits." I was about to talk to very high achievers, let us roll the dice and see if these incredibly successful people had their Habits that others could make part of their lives. I decided to ask each person the same question. One question and one question only. "If you could instantly instill in a child, one habit, what would it be and why?" The first answer was perfect. The second one was great. As I listened to each answer, I thought to myself, "What would my life be like if these habits were a part of who I am?" I also notice that many of these successful people from many different walks of life had the same habits.

Although I realized my videos were quite good and you can still see them at www.Envision.tv, I saw something more. As a book, the reader can skim through it and land on a Habit and say, "That is a Habit I want to make a part of me." They would spend the time, instill the Habit, and once it is part of them, they can flip through the pages and find the next one.

With the idea in hand, I set out to find 100 extremely high achievers from many walks of life to contribute to our first book. I was genuinely amazed by the extraordinary people that contributed to the first 1 Habit™ book. I have such gratitude for them believing enough in what I was doing to join. The first book became an Amazon Bestseller shortly after we published it.

The 1 Habit Movement

Shortly after the original 1 Habit became a Bestseller, I realized that the processes I put in place that let me organize these 100, high achieving individuals was uncommon but highly effective. More importantly, the resulting book that I created from these processes had become something that was having a significant impact on people's lives.

I sat back and watched as the incredible contributors to the book each were telling their own stories about how they became a part of the book and how excited they each were about its potential. One contributor emailed me and said, "Steve, what you have created is now more than a book. It has become a movement."

The Power of Collaboration

One of the most exciting parts of putting together the first 1 Habit book was spending each day talking with some of the most inspiring and creative people on the planet. Even more exciting was the fact that there were more Habits, then we could fit into one book.

I saw groupings of Habits that fit for particular demographics of people. It was at that time that I decided 1 Habit would become a series of books. I would take the processes I create for book one and replicate that for each new book.

The bottleneck would be finding the 100 people in each demographic of each book. I quickly fixed this by teaming up with an extraordinary co-author for each new book in the series.

Each co-author will be an expert from a specific group or field. Co-Authors organize the contributors and follow our marketing plan to get the books in as many people's hands as possible in a very organic way.

As of this writing, we have five new 1 Habit books in process with five incredible Co-Authors. My goal is to publish once a month, each for particular groups of people.

The book you are now reading is the second book in the 1 Habit series. I teamed up with the extraordinary Lynda Sunshine West to create a 1 Habit book for and about Women Action Takers. I think this book will have a massive impact on not just the Women that read it, but also the ones that came to together to contribute to it.

Steven Samblis – Creator of 1 Habit™ and Founder of Envision Media Partners.

HOW TO USE THIS BOOK

How to use your 1 Habit Book

After you have read this Introduction, read the chapter "How to Make a Habit Your Own. This will give you the tools to install a habit inside yourself, so it is a part of who you are.

Next, skim through the book and stop on a habit. Decide if the Habit would enhance your life. If it would follow the steps to make the habit part of who you are.

Once you own that Habit and it is a part of what you do every day, skim through the book again and find your next Habit.

The habits from our 100 high achieving contributors are in no particular order. We did this purposefully to add some magic and serendipity to your journey.

Instill just 1 Habit, and it can change your life forever. Instill five, and you may change the World!

HOW TO MAKE A HABIT YOUR OWN

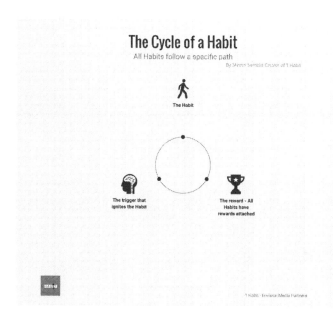

The Cycle of a Habit
All Habits follow a specific path

By Steven Semple Creator of 1 Habit

The Habit

The trigger that
ignites the Habit

The reward - All
Habits have
rewards attached

There is a cycle to all Habits. The cycle has three steps.

1st step: The Habit. It is the behavior you want to change, add, or remove.

2nd Step: The Reward. It is the payoff you get from the Habit.

3rd Step: The Trigger. It is the thing that makes you perform the Habit.

With a small amount of work, you can build a new Habit that requires little effort to maintain. After a great deal of research, we offer the top 11 things you need to keep in mind to make a Habit part of who you are.

1. Let Your Habit Find You. To do this, skim through the chapters and stop when you feel you are ready. Read the Habit and the 'Why". If this is the one for you, it's time to begin practicing it every day until you own it.

2. Write Your Habit Down – Once you have your Habit, write it down. Not just the Habit but also your "Why." Knowing the reason why is as important as the Habit itself. Understand why you are instilling the Habit from the start. Writing the Habit and the "Why" makes your ideas more clear and focuses you on the results you are looking for. Use a 3x5 card and write the Habit several times and place the card around places where you will see them every day. Write a smaller version and keep it in your purse or wallet. Once you own the Habit, you can put these away.

3. Work On It Every Day– You will need to work on your Habit every day. Repetition is essential if you want to

make a habit stick. If you're going to start reading every day, have a book ready every day for your first month. Reading a couple of times a week will make it harder to form the Habit.

4. Take a Month – A month is a perfect amount of time to commit to a change since it easily fits in your calendar.

5. Set Reminders – Set up reminders to enact your Habit each day, or you might miss a few days. The best way is to set it up on your phone calendar. Have a daily reminder that pops up every day.

6. Form Triggers – This is a term from NLP (Neuro-Linguistic Programming). Triggers call forth behaviors (not thoughts or feelings). A trigger is a ritual you use right before executing your Habit. If your Habit was to reflect on the days as it ends, you could practice snapping your fingers each time before you begin. This action wires the Habit to your brain and helps it to become an automatic action.

7. Get a Mentor – Spend more time with people who do the things you want to do. If you're going to lose weight and get in better shape, hang out with people who work out and are at their best health-wise.

8. Get a Friend to Hold You Accountable – Find a friend who will support you and keep you motivated if you feel like giving up. (This is one of our favorites)

9. Remove Temptation – Change your World so it won't tempt you in the first month. If your Habit is to eat

healthy every day, Remove junk food from your house. This way, you won't find yourself struggling later as you look at your temptations right in front of you.

Side note...

Keep It Simple And Don't Try to Be Perfect – Don't try to change your world in one day. It is easy to take on too much at one time. Start small and build, and do be afraid to fail. Habits will come but not all at once and not entirely. Expect bumps in the road along the way.

ARE YOU A HAPPY ACHIEVER?

For years, my life was focused on being a high achiever. Success was all I could think about. And success meant one thing and one thing only, how much money I made.

Throughout my journey, I would go out of my way to meet respected leaders in business, culture, and social change to learn their secrets and apply them to my success.

But, as I set out to create 1 Habit, I learned something even more amazing. It turns out, my desire to achieve was on target, but I measured it all wrong—in dollars and cents.

I realized, no matter how much money I made, I wasn't as happy as I thought I'd be; there was always going to be someone making more.

One day it dawned on me, I needed to redefine what success meant to me. Money was not the right measurement of success. Money may be how others measure my success. Why should I give them this power?

I soon realized that happiness is how I wanted to measure my success. My happiness is something I am in control of. The way to reach happiness is to perform at your highest level in all plains of existence. The people that came together as contributors for 1 Habit all did this. These amazing people were all operating at the highest levels, Emotionally, Spiritual, their physical character, the way they live, and of course, financially. Happiness through the balance of performing and living at your peak in all those areas of their lives.

From that day forward, I would keep score based on the time I spent with my family, my friends, my hobbies, exploring the world, and realizing my passions and dreams.

I knew what I wanted to do now but did not know what to call this new category of a person that achieved highly at all levels and, as a result, were some of the happiest people on the planet.

Ask, and you shall receive

Whenever I have a question or a problem, I put it out that, and the universe always seems to give me the answers when I need them.

I was sitting with a friend who started out creating marketing campaigns for companies like ATT. He moved from there to head up a company that produces the marketing campaign for all the major Hollywood studios. If you saw a movie in the last 20 years, there is a high likelihood that Mike Tankel was part of the reason you walked into that theater.

I told Mike about my new way of keeping score in life with happiness, not money. I no longer wanted to be a singular high achiever. I was something more. This thing was "the" more.

With little effort, it rolled off Mike's tongue. "You don't want to be a High Achiever. You want to be a Happy Achiever". And there we have it. A "High Achiever."

So now I ask you, my dear reader. How do you keep score in life? More importantly, how do you want to keep score in life?

I hope you will join us and live your life to the fullest on all plains of existence. I hope you, too, will become a Happy Achiever!

Steven Samblis

Creator of 1 Habit™

DEFINITION OF HABIT

Habit: A behavior pattern acquired by frequent repetition or physiologic exposure that shows itself in regularity or increased facility of performance.

1

PAT YOURSELF ON THE BACK -- OFTEN - LYNDA SUNSHINE WEST

The Habit: Pat Yourself On the Back -- Often

By Lynda Sunshine West - Mastermind/Accountability Coach, Executive Film Producer, Wish Man Movie, co-author 1 Habit for Women Action Takers

Why: Have you ever heard the saying, "You're your own worst enemy?"

Often we are so much better at mentally beating ourselves down than we are at lifting ourselves up.

Do you agree?

Think of a time when you did something that you were mad at yourself for doing. Did you beat yourself up mentally?

Did it happen today, yesterday, or last week? Did it happen several times today?

With so much negativity in the world, one thing we do have control over is our thoughts.

Although I mentioned that you should 'pat yourself on the back,' what I mean is that you should practice saying good things to yourself and become your own best cheerleader, not your own worst enemy.

Having grown up in a volatile, physically, mentally, and verbally abusive household caused negative thoughts to continually swirl around in my head.

At the ripe old age of 51, I looked at my life and said, "Is this all there is? There's gotta be more to life than this."

You see, those first 51 years of my life I was trapped in my own prison. My mind was filled with constant negativity.

As I was driving to work one day, I asked myself questions like, "What is the purpose of this planet? What is the purpose of me being here?" When I got to the office, I saw a message on Facebook that said, "I'm a life coach. I took a break, and I'm ready to get back into it. I'm looking for five women who want to change their life."

Wow! I felt like she was talking to me. Even though I didn't know her, I believed that she would change my life. So I raised my hand, and I jumped all in. It was the first time in my life that I raised my hand to change me.

I had been a people-pleaser my whole life, and the

opportunity to become someone different was very intriguing, yet scary. I was willing to take the chance and do something different.

I am so grateful to myself for saying 'yes' to me.

What does this have to do with patting yourself on the back?

Well, I spent decades with people saying negative things to me, and it got to the point that I learned how to say negative things to myself faster than they could. I believed all of the negativity, and I had become my own worst enemy.

By working with my life coach, she taught me how to become my own best cheerleader, and I started cheering for myself regularly. It completely changed the way I see and talk to myself.

What patting myself on the back has done for me is that it's given me strength and courage to no longer require other people to support me emotionally or mentally. This is HUGE because it's given me the strength and courage to step out without a crutch.

It's given me the confidence to stand up and say I am here and ready to change your world when you're ready.

It's given me the strength to keep pushing forward even when it feels like things are failing. I've learned to fail forward because my cheerleader keeps me going.

How do you pat yourself on the back?

You look at your accomplishments, and you say, "WOW! I am amazing. Look at what I did."

It may feel weird at first, but that will change. You'll learn to love it and to say it more frequently. It will become second-nature to congratulate yourself on a job well done. It will help you to gain confidence and belief in yourself like no one else has ever believed in you.

After all, you are the most important human in your life. Others will come and go, but you will always be with you.

As you go through life and do things that you are proud of, remember to pat yourself on the back. You don't have to do it out loud, but if you feel confident enough, I strongly urge you to say it out loud to yourself and others.

It's time for you to step into your power and live your best life as a brilliant and amazing person you are.

The Un-Habit: Stop Saying Yes to Everyone

Why: Yes is an awesome word but, when used too often, can be draining.

Have you ever said 'yes' to someone and then regretted saying it because you 1) don't have enough time to fulfill your new obligation, 2) don't want to do what you said 'yes' to, 3) meant to say 'no,' but 'yes' came out of your mouth?

I hear ya. Been there, done that.

As a reformed people-pleaser, I know all too well how

hard saying 'no' can be, but also know how important it is.

Saying 'no' is a way of setting boundaries, of saying, "I'm here, and this is what I want and what I don't want."

Here are three easy examples of how to say 'no' without saying 'no.'

"Thank you so much for wanting my help. I appreciate it. I'm going to pass this time because I'm afraid I won't be able to devote enough time to your project and give it my all. I'll try to think of someone else who can help you."

"I'm honored you'd like me to help you with that. Your trust in me means a lot. While I love what you do and want to support you, I'm concentrating on building my business right now and need to stay focused. I'm on the verge of a breakthrough. I'll let you know if I think of someone who can help you."

"Oh, man. I want to help you with that because I believe in everything you do, but I'm unable to help you at this time. Please check in with me in a couple of months. I should be further along with my projects so I can give you my all. In the meantime, I'll let you know if I think of someone else who can help you."

These examples will enable you to say no without feeling weird about it (I used to feel weird saying no, but I now use these phrases (and others) to make it much easier for me).

What happens when we say 'yes' to others is we are saying 'no' to ourselves.

Saying 'yes' can create feelings of regret, tension, frustration, aggravation, resentment, etc.

Learning to say 'no' and creating your boundaries will help you gain a lot of confidence to step up for yourself when you want to and need to.

ABOUT LYNDA: Lynda Sunshine West is a Mastermind/Accountability Coach who helps driven women entrepreneurs gain confidence to ask for their worth, clarity to attract clients TO them, and focus to get faster results.

Having grown up in a volatile, physically, mentally and verbally abusive alcoholic household and marrying someone just like her dad, Lynda's voice was stifled far too long. It left her feeling suppressed, ignored and judged, which made her shut down.

At the age of 51, she found a life coach who helped her discover that she has value and that it was time for her to share her voice and speak out loud. In doing so, she was met with praise, recognition and acknowledgment.

That led her to creating the Women Action Takers Mastermind/Accountability Program helping women entrepreneurs 2X and 3X their business. She no longer sits in the back of the room, but now speaks on stages, interviews stars on the red carpet, makes tv and podcast appearances, and created the Women Action Takers Podcast.

Lynda proudly donates 10% of her profits to The Giving Angels, a 501(c)(3) nonprofit whose mission is to get homeless veterans off the streets and into homes.

2

BE CONSISTENT IN A TIMELY RESPONSE (24-28 HOURS) - DR. AMY NOVOTNY

Habit: Be consistent in a timely response (24-28 hours)

Dr. Amy Novotny – Founder the PABR Institute™

Why: We know that communication is essential to the health of a relationship. We often respond quickly to an initial interaction with a new acquaintance, connection or client because we are eager to see where it leads. We put our best selves forward and demonstrate good communication skills initially. The relationship is off to a good start at this point but it's still in the honeymoon phase. The problem comes when we return to our daily life after an event or after that initial interaction when we get bogged down in other tasks and priorities. Responses to these new connections become more and more delayed and even drop off. We can change this though by developing a new habit--one of being consistent with a timely response to all communications. Ideally, responding within the day is best to demonstrate the value you place on the relationship. The outer limit of this habit of a 24-48 hour response time still sets a great tone with the new connection or acquaintance. It demonstrates a level of care, respect, and value that leads to deeper relationships. This can be accomplished by setting aside 15-20 minutes at the end of a work day and at the beginning of a new day to respond to emails, texts and phone calls.

This habit can change your life in a few ways. We all have many tasks hanging over our heads each day, whether they are work, personal or family-related. Those unresolved tasks add stress to our lives and muddy up our minds. If we respond to communications more efficiently, it removes some of those tasks off our plate and our mind can free up for other work-related or life-related activities that require focus. The relief is palpable.

You can also benefit from this habit through what it does for your reputation. That person receiving your communication will view you differently because you took action and responded quicker than others. They will appreciate your attention to their needs. Your trustworthiness will increase and you will become known as a reliable and responsible person, one in which others want to interact with. Even if the communication is a simple message that explains you need a week to write a full response, it will work wonders on the relationship because it sets expectations and a level of respect for both parties.

You might also get opportunities that others won't receive because they waited too long. It's hard to know the full extent of this benefit but any door that opens, gives you more choices and options of how you want your life to unfold.

The Un-Habit: Being independent as possible

Why: We love the feeling of accomplishment, especially if we conquered something on our own for the first time. However, this can be a detriment to ourselves if we don't let go of this habit of independence. There can be many reasons why we attempt to do as much as possible ourselves. It could be related to finances, understaffing, lack of knowledge by others, etc. We not only hurt ourselves when we don't change, but we also delay the impact we can have on the world.

When we pursue our purpose in life, we often want to share it with society through a business, a job or a hobby. We might think that if we do it all ourselves, we will get great recognition for what we have accomplished. This can be a slow arduous process. We can reach more people faster when we bring others into our world to help us. If, for instance, your purpose is to get people out of pain through a special method or technique, then enlisting the help of others in building that business will help you serve more people. You can choose to do your own books, finances, marketing, social media ads, etc; or you can hire a bookkeeper, an accountant, a marketer and a business coach to allow them to do their love and passion while you spend your time on developing your pain-relieving techniques. This is a hard step to take and habit to break when you are first starting out, but it's worth it. It will also free you up to train others in your specialty so more people benefit from your knowledge or skill.

The development of a team can change your life through having a community that you can rely on. Your message will expand faster because now you have several people wanting the success of the idea or business. They can share your passion to their network of people and it grows from there. The stress you had trying to accomplish all the varied tasks of running a business or pursuing your passion can be alleviated because more skilled people in those tasks can take over while allowing you to focus your attention on your skillset and purpose. Everyone wins.

ABOUT DR. AMY: Dr. Amy Novotny founded the PABR Institute™ in 2018 with the mission to provide pain, stress and anxiety relief to those who seek a naturalistic form of treatment when other treatment methods have fallen short. Her unique approach comes from her experience treating in a variety of settings and with a wide range of patient populations over the past 10 years. Her background in orthopedics, sports, geriatrics, balance disor-

ders, nerve injuries, and most recently, chronic pain; and influences from coursework at the Postural Restoration Institute gave her the foundation to develop this treatment method to address a wide variety of painful and restrictive conditions. These techniques have helped countless clients cancel scheduled orthopedic surgeries, including knee replacements, disc herniation removal and fusions in the neck and low back, rotator cuff tear repairs, and ACL tear reconstructions. She co-authored an Amazon #1 Best-Selling book Don't Quit: Stories of Persistence, Courage and Faith, which shares her journey on how and why she developed the PABR Method™. Her ability to speak French and Spanish has allowed her to communicate with and help various clients from all around the world, including France, Mexico, Central America and South America. Dr. Amy now works with clients one-on-one in her office or virtually online and presents around the US to various mastermind meetings, corporate wellness meetings, and business seminars to teach others how to gain control over their bodies to eliminate pain and ward off the physical effects of stress and anxiety. She has used this method to stay pain- and injury-free for the later half of her endurance career including 40+ marathons, 10 ultra marathons (including two 100 milers), and an Ironman Triathlon. In her spare time, Dr. Amy volunteers for the nonprofit, Arizona Highways PhotoScapes, and she photographs wildlife and landscapes all over the world that has led to several of her images being being featured in art galleries and chosen as Photos of the Day, most notably National Geographic "Your Shot World Top Photo of the Day. "

3

VALUE EVERYONE ON YOUR TEAM - SUSAN O'MALLEY MD

The Habit: Value everyone on your team

By Susan O'Malley MD -
Former Emergency Room Doctor, Entrepreneur, Author

Why: Your team is bigger than you think. We tend to think of our team as people who report directly to us. The reality is anyone who does a job that enables you to do your job is on your team.

That means the janitor is on your team; the UPS driver is on your team; the secretary in your department and yes, maybe even the pizza delivery man are all on your team. Because if they didn't do their job, you couldn't do yours. They all bring value and they all deserve to be recognized and acknowledged.

When I worked in the emergency room, I always said hello to the janitor. We didn't even speak the same language. I'd smile at him and he'd smile at me. If I was sitting at the desk, I'd hand him the trash can so he didn't have to reach for it.

He used to carry hard candy in his pocket and always gave me a piece of candy. Why – because he appreciated that someone at the top saw him and appreciated his contribution. Everyone was so busy and no one spoke to the janitor, but if the janitor didn't keep the ER clean, we couldn't have seen patients.

If housekeeping didn't come and wipe up the blood after a trauma, we couldn't take care of the next trauma. If UPS doesn't deliver the package to your client when they say they will, you can lose the account. If the pizza delivery man shows up an hour late with cold pizza, you're too hungry to concentrate.

Another point to consider when talking about valuing everyone is follow-through. As an emergency room doctor, I never asked anybody to do anything that I had not or would not have done myself. And when I got the result, I tracked that person down to let them know.

Remember when I asked you to get that chest x-ray? Well, here is what pneumonia looks like. We're going to admit him to the hospital. Remember when I asked you to draw the blood on the patient in room two? He's anemic – I wouldn't have guessed. Thanks – I appreciate that.

It made people feel like they were part of the team.

Because they were. The tech making $10 an hour, the emergency room doctor and everyone in-between were all on the same team. The staff used to tell me I was their favorite ER doctor. How did that happen? Because I treated everyone the way I would have wanted to be treated. Nothing more.

And you can be everyone's favorite leader as well. Just remember, don't confuse leadership with being in charge. Treat them as distant cousins, not identical twins. Because it doesn't matter if you're in medicine, in business or anywhere in-between, we all want the same thing. We want to be seen, we want to be heard and we want to be appreciated.

The Un-Habit: Stop comparing yourself to other people

Why: When you compare yourself to someone else or your business to another, you only see what they want you to see. You never get the full picture. It can leave you feeling inadequate and like a failure. Social media has compounded this problem. I've never seen such a parade of success as I have seen on Facebook!

People might be as smart or successful as they would have you believe, or they may not. Either way, when you compare yourself to the story you see or hear, you set yourself up for internal failure.

I left the emergency room and opened my med spa business when I was fifty years old. There were no entrepreneurs in my family and I had no business training, so I really didn't know what I was doing. "If you build it they will come" may have worked for Kevin Costner's *Field of Dreams* character, but it doesn't work in business. It took me about six months and a dwindling bank account to figure that out.

That's when I started going to networking events and meeting other business owners. After the introductory pleasantries, the question "How's business" always seemed to come up. Everyone would smile and let you know how well they were doing. My brand new business was failing and I was scrambling for ideas on how to salvage it. I was getting more and more depressed going to meetings and comparing my business to all those successful people.

What is wrong with me? Why can't I make this work?

One evening, I decided to be honest. When the question came up, rather than nodding and smiling, I decided to tell the truth. "Could be better" I said. Imagine my surprise when other business owners started admitting their struggles as well.

I had spent all that time comparing myself to other business owners and feeling like a failure because I thought they had it all figured out. When I shared my struggle, I opened the door for them to share theirs as well.

I learned two valuable lessons: Not only don't compare myself to other people, but don't confuse struggle with failure. We all struggle; it doesn't mean you're failing.

About Dr. Susan O'Malley: Former emergency room doctor, entrepreneur and author, Dr. Susan O'Malley combines leadership and life lessons with stories from the trenches to help powerful women lead more effectively.

In her book *Tough Cookies Don't Crumble: Turn Set-Backs into Success,* she outlines strategies that transformed her from college drop-out and secretary to emergency room doctor and entrepreneur.

After leaving the ER at age fifty, Dr. O'Malley opened Madison Med Spa, a cosmetic practice dedicated to helping women navigate aging without surgery. After seventeen years in service to the women of Connecticut and beyond, Dr. O'Malley closed Madison Med Spa and is transitioning careers yet again.

Her firsthand experience of helping women empower themselves at the Med Spa was the basis for her TEDx Talk, *How Beauty Secrets Turned into Secret Weapons.*

In an attempt to help aspiring TEDx speakers take their place on the red circle, Dr. O'Malley has taken the lessons learned from her three year journey to the TEDx stage and distilled them into a soon to be released online course – TEDx: From the Trenches to the Stage.

A sought after keynote speaker, Dr. O'Malley has also been featured in Entrepreneur Magazine, FOX News and multiple podcasts and magazine articles. She is a member of the National Speakers Association and past president of the Connecticut chapter.

Dr. O'Malley also served six years on the Board of Directors of the Madison Chamber of Commerce where she started and was chairperson of the Women in Business Committee.

4

CELEBRATE THE SMALL WINS AND GIVE YOURSELF SOME CREDIT EVERY DAY - NICHOLE B. CLARK

The Habit: Celebrate the small wins and give yourself some credit every day.

By Nichole B. Clark - Author, Speaker & Coach

Why: As a mother of six, I have had my fair share of potty-training and trying to get my kids to behave the way I want. Any mother knows that the process is not exactly fun and includes a learning curve. It is also different with every child, so even if you have it "figured out" with one kid, the next is not guaranteed to be so easy.

Teachers also utilize many techniques to motivate kids to perform their best at school.

Some kids are motivated by a simple sticker chart. Others

like candy or money, while some will settle for a simple "good job" from our mouths.

Even puppies learn quickly when they are given proper incentives.

Yet when it comes to adulting or getting things done, the grand majority of women I know have no idea how to motivate themselves to get things done effectively. We have become so obsessed with doing and hurrying to the next thing that we rarely stop and celebrate the small wins of life.

After potty training, one of my children years ago, I decided that I might benefit from the simple idea of rewarding myself for small achievements. While I didn't get an actual sticker chart, I chose instead to stop and give myself credit for the little things I accomplished each day.

I got into the habit of celebrating my wins, no matter how small.

The result has been nothing short of amazing.

The simple act of doing a happy dance after getting the dishes cleaned, or proclaiming, "I am amazing" after putting all the laundry away made housekeeping a lot more enjoyable. Treating myself to a nice dinner or a night out with friends after taking more baby steps towards my dreams of becoming an entrepreneur made the journey fun.

I found that as I celebrated my baby wins throughout the day, I wanted to do more things to celebrate. I began taking more action toward my dreams. Somehow the mountains I was moving became so much more enjoyable when I celebrated each pebble moved along the way.

I quickly found my self-confidence skyrocketing, my feelings of self-worth blooming, and my anxiety decreasing. The more I gave myself credit for the little things; the less *little* things seemed to be. Rather than getting stressed out over my mile-long to-do list and beating myself up over not being able to cross every single thing off, I began feeling amazing for getting even one or two things done.

So, get into the habit of rewarding yourself for the little things you do daily.

You can make a sticker chart or a calendar to document your achievements. You could give yourself a monetary award, or even plan an elaborate vacation, but start today to give yourself some credit. I promise the more that you do that, the happier, more fulfilled you will be. The motivation you seek to "get things done" will no longer be an issue! Happy achieving friend- you deserve a hug!

The Un-Habit: Stop Feeding Your Inner Critic

Why: I used to have a to-do list a mile long. It would've been impossible for anyone to get all the things done in a day, yet somehow I expected myself too. At the end of the day, I would cross a minimal amount of the things off and then mentally beat myself up over each of the remaining items. I felt like a failure like somehow that list determined my worth or how successful I was.

My inner critic would have a field day, making sure I knew how pathetic I was.

When I didn't hit my goals the moment I thought I would or didn't get as much done as I thought I should, it was there to beat me down and make fun.

I heard it over my physical lack after comparing myself to everyone else's highlight reel on social media. My hair and clothing and body type didn't make the cut.

It was terrible when it came to my mothering skills. Every other mother seemed to be doing such a better job than me. They would take their kids on fun outings out of town, while I was barely surviving a trip to the grocery store. The other mothers always seemed to find time to volunteer at the kids' school, while I was lucky if my kids made it to school on time.

When it came to my house, I was yet again, not measuring up. I heard the critic incessantly. "You don't even know how to clean grout between tile!" "How do you expect your kids or your husband to like your cooking, it is mediocre at best." "Do you really think that you can get that stain out of those clothes? You've never been able to before!"

Every seemingly small mistake or a mishap in my life would result in feeling like I wasn't good enough.

In pretty much every area of my life, I felt like a failure, and my inner critic was calling all the shots.

However, that all changed the minute, I learned that I

could choose to stop feeding the inner critic. I could ignore it's taunting and choose to feed another side of me instead.

I learned that I had an inner cheerleader that had been hibernating for much longer than the winter.

I wondered which one is stronger, the inner critic or cheerleader?

I found it depends on which one we feed.

In other words, it matters which one we listen to and give heed too.

The more we avoid the bullying of the critic and lean into the support of our inner guidance system, the more we find ourselves feeling fulfilled and less of a failure.

Get into the daily habit of ignoring the inner critic and feeding the cheerleader.

Each time you hear the bully come out to play, quietly invite them to leave the playground of your mind. Becoming aware of them and choosing to let them go will leave you feeling empowered and excited about life.

Learning to hear the cheer from within has made me a much more accomplished and happy person today. The bully will always be there, but their words no longer mean anything to me. I hope the same can happen for you too!

ABOUT NICHOLE: Nichole Clark is, first and foremost, a mother and a spouse. She and her husband, Nathan, have been married for 17 years and have six kids together. Nichole is the author of The 10-Minute Refresh for Moms, and Founder of More than Moms (a Facebook group for every mother no matter their age or stage). She and her husband love to coach others and help them uproot their limiting beliefs at the subconscious level so they can grow, glow, and overflow. They have several challenges and courses to help people live their best lives and get out of survival mode.

5

BUILD CONNECTED COMMUNITIES - KYM GLASS

The Habit: Build connected communities

By Kym Glass - Soft Skills Consultant, Award Winning Speaker and Best Selling Author

Why:From my experience in building connected communities of over 50,000 people across multiple organizations, it has shown me how important COURAGE is to women executives and business owners.

Courage doesn't mean that you don't feel fear, it means that you move through the fear with your focus on the goals and dreams you are working to accomplish.

In my book Unshakeable Courage, I discuss The Seven Promises of Courage that I created based on my experiences and now has helped so many women achieve their personal and professional goals.

Specifically, The Seven Promises of Courage are:

C – Confidence – Believe in Yourself.

O – Ownership – Be in the Driver's Seat of Your Own Life.

U – Unstoppable – Trust Your Inner Power.

R – Relationships – Create Your Connected Community.

A – Action – Take a Different Action for a Different Result.

G – Gratitude – The Gateway to Your Desires.

E - Empowered – Helping Others from Who You Are.

Through courage, I have helped others create and build connected communities larger and more successful than we had ever thought possible.

A sushi lunch with a woman business owner and friend in one of my connected communities was the start of building a 7 figure entrepreneurial business and a team of over 15,000 in less than three years. I was really ignorance on fire with a fantastic experience and I simply started by driving every day on my lunch hour to the local Chick Fil A ™, sitting in my car and using their free WIFI to reach out to my connected community about a product that had helped my life switch come back on after some health issues.

Another connected community introduction was meeting a wonderful woman and business owner and staying connected. Fast forward 15 years, she was the connection that suggested that I should apply to speak on the TEDx platform and share my idea "Break Free from Generational Patterns to Create an Unlimited Future." Shortly after sharing my story on the TEDx platform, it was approved as an idea worth sharing and is now featured on the TEDx YouTube channel.

Relationships, you never know why or when you meet people. I remember as a little girl, my mom always told my sister and I, "There is always a reason or a season why you meet people, be kind always!"

My mom's words to this day continue to be an impact on the relationships and connection that I have been so fortunate to create and build connected communities.

By lifting and supporting other women, we can continue to build connected community and celebrate exceptional wins together!

The Un-Habit: Stop listening to the opinions of others that do not serve your highest good.

Why: By listening to the opinions of others that do not serve your highest good, you begin to internalize and create fear, anxiety and people pleasing.

One of the main reasons for me living in so much fear in one particular area of my life is because I was conditioned from a very young age by growing up in a religious cult and I lost confidence in that area of my life.

I had been so conditioned early on and as I grew older, I continued buying into the cult leader's negative opinions of me and what I should be doing to please them and their continuous demands.

I listened to what the cult leader's opinions were of me because I believed that surely they must know me better than I knew myself.

After my escape of 35 years, I realized what a crazy and ridiculous way to give away your power to someone that will manipulate you for their needs, time, their noise, etc., above your own dreams, desires and goals.

You know how we often hear our children are our best teachers? I remember when my daughter Meredith was in pre-school. She was playing with a friend and Meredith decided she wanted to play something different than her friend. Her friend quickly said, "If you don't play this with me, then I'm not going to be your best friend." Without skipping a beat in the conversation, Meredith quickly replied, "I'm my own best friend!" and that was the end of the conversation and they went on to play separate activities, but also remained friends.

About Kym: With a career that spans 20+ years in the corporate experience and over 17 years as an entrepreneur and business owner, Kym Glass has built multiple connected communities in excess of 50,000 people.

DURING HER CORPORATE CAREER, she was a finalist for the Women In Technology award presented by Ebby Halliday on behalf of the YWCA. As an entrepreneur and business owner, she was a finalist for the Best Business Connector in Dallas and an Honoree presented at the International Association of Women Gala.

Kym is a TEDx speaker and her idea of "Break Free from Generational Patterns to Create An Unlimited Future" is now featured on the TEDx You Tube Channel.

Her book, Unshakeable Courage message and mission is to help others Face Reality, Release Your Fears and Live with Power! She shares her personal journey of being raised in a religious cult and overcoming mental, emotional and bullying abuse. She shares the roadmap she created along her journey to escape after 35 years to protect her daughter and ensure that the generational pattern was broken. Her roadmap featured in her book through The Seven Promises of Courage is powerful to help others overcome fear in their personal or professional life. She is currently on a national speaking, book signing, and media tour sharing her Unshakeable Courage message and most recently appeared on CBS Great Day Washington in Washington, DC.

Kym shares her "Unshakeable Courage" message of her personal and business experiences from which she has built three proven growth systems so you can achieve your journey to success:

"The Seven Promises of Courage"

"Take your Business and Voice from whisper To ROARRR!" ™

"Soft Skills Strategies for Bottom Line Results"

Kym Glass is the CEO of Soft Skills Strategies a consulting and speaking agency that leverages soft skills to create surprising bottom line results.

She is a Soft Skills Consultant, Award Winning Speaker and Best Selling Author. She is always passionate to learn more about you, your business and how she can best support you.

6

LEAVE PERFECTION TO MARTHA STEWART! (AND BY THE WAY, SHE'S NOT PERFECT EITHER!) - SUSAN D SHARP

The Habit: Leave perfection to Martha Stewart! (And by the way, she's not perfect either!)

By Susan D Sharp - Artist, Speaker, Author of Mid-Life Wisdom and 1 Habit.

Why: There are 168 Hours in your week. You don't have the time to pursue perfection-- it's overrated and unnecessary. Women action takers can get things done without sacrificing quality or needing to agonize about things that don't significantly affect the desired outcome. As Confucius said, "Better a diamond with a flaw than a pebble without." You're already a diamond, ladies, so trust and love yourself enough not to get caught up in the unimportant!

I knew a bride once who held up every other aspect of

her wedding because she debated for seven weeks about three different shades of salmon for her color palette. Since the venue with the most comfort and amenities for her guests wouldn't repaint the walls to accommodate her savoy salmon color palette, she selected a cramped space without adequate room for everyone, and most of the guests left early. Sure it was beautiful, but we don't remember the beauty; we remember having to walk a half-mile in heels to our cars and waiting 30 minutes to get a cocktail. What's wrong with that picture? I love details; I love the touches that make my events, paintings, and books unique. But special can't come at the expense of doing, and it's not more important than people.

One thing I admire about genuinely successful people is how quickly they can prioritize tasks. They can delegate and change plans without missing a beat. Perfection is often rigid and unbending; it usually cannot stand when adversity comes. It does not know how to compromise, and it often makes an enemy of others. Action-takers understand Voltaire when he said, "The best is the enemy of the good."

I throw a formal brunch every Christmas for 12 of my favorite women. I use my great-grandmother's 24k gold-rimmed bone china that she painted in the 1910s. It makes me happy to have a connection with my family and my heritage. I arrange my flowers in the center of the table, I coordinate the linens, and I have a color palette-- salmon, by the way, happens to be one of my favorites-- and I make sure everything goes together. It's the one time a year I do it up big, and I love the details. I cook several courses and often make gourmet desserts, of which even Martha would be proud. But--the linens are not more important than the guests, the food is not more important than taking time to make everyone feel special or to soak in what they've done or experienced since the last brunch. Perfection is not the goal, even though I love trying to make it unique. Perfection makes us lose sight of ourselves and others. Perfection cannot see the difference between the pebble and the diamond.

By the time you eat, sleep, and work, your 168 hours have dwindled considerably. What do you do with that remaining undesignated time? Women action takers fill it with meaningful relationships, education, fun, and enrichment. We look to the future instead of just til the end of the day. We plan, we dream, we are decisive about what is important and impatient with things that are not. Use your 168 hours this week wisely and leave perfection to Martha Stewart.

The Un-Habit: Stop comparing yourself to other women!

Why: Only you have your unique set of skills, experiences, family, outlook, temperament, etc. There is only one you! When you compare yourself to other women, you negate your uniqueness! It's like standing at a bakery counter and endlessly comparing a croissant to a brioche--they're both wonderful, so stop analyzing yourself to death and enjoy who you are--even your flakey layers!

I'm an expert at the flakey layers--I have a corny sense of humor, I've said the wrong thing, I've tripped in public, I've given a whole speech with lipstick on my teeth, I've even been on the jumbo screen at a baseball game singing the national anthem when I knocked some speakers and monitors down. Between my depth perception and living in the moment, I'm aware of my flaws, and they are many. But the flip side of that is that I am compassionate toward others, I laugh at myself easily, I have people that look out for me, and I always have great stories for when I speak! Oh, how boring it would be to live a flawless life! I'm thankful that I'll never know!

It's important to stop comparing yourself with other women because there's the only one you and you are amazing! I think girls need to learn this lesson early when they're gawking at the cover models and celebrities that are stick thin or have perfect skin. Between the airbrushing and the retouching of photographs, those celebrities aren't even real!

Love the one you're with, and you're with YOU, so love YOU. Find the flip side of what you consider to be your flaws and embrace them--see them as your assets instead. All you have to do is to change your stinkin' thinkin', and everything looks different!

When you stop comparing yourself to others--which, ladies, is passing judgment--you are free to love yourself and others without feeling threatened or being petty or snarky. Oh, that women would support instead of judge each other! There's so much freedom that comes when you let that go and think about more worthy ideas!

Imagine walking into a fancy affair where there are lots of beautiful people in a beautiful location. Instead of obsessing about your clothes, your weight, and your hair, what if you were freed up to see the architecture, the skyline, the chandeliers and to hear the beautiful music. What about approaching a group and introducing your-self instead of wallowing in the corner because you don't think you're as put together as the others? What about breaking a destructive cycle of shame and guilt and nega-tivity with the idea that YOU'RE ALWAYS AS GOOD AS EVERYBODY ELSE, period.

About Susan: Susan Sharp is an abstract artist, author of Mid-Life Wisdom, and a speaker with a passion for understanding our creative potential and motivations. Her blend of humor and ease of presentation makes her a sought-after speaker. Susan speaks about her career in the arts, the artist's workspace and its importance in creativity, her Midwest upbringing, her career in (and departure from) teaching in higher education, and the desire to see all people—especially those who don't consider themselves creative—let go of limiting beliefs and blocks to their greatness.

Through a combination of years of personal study on

creativity as well as her own involvement in numerous creative pursuits (art, music, design, directing, playwriting, craft, voiceovers, writing), Susan understands that creativity doesn't just happen—it is cultivated, nurtured and practiced. Habits become the cornerstone of an artist's work. Susan's best habit is currently featured in the book, 1 Habit: 100 Habits from the happiest achievers on the planet, by Steve Samblis.

Susan's art was recently featured on the set of Season 7 of Orange is The New Black and her children's book series, The Farty Boys, will be on Amazon very soon.

7

RECLAIM - REBUILD - RADIATE - ROBYN JORDAN

The Habit: Reclaim - Rebuild - Radiate

By Robyn Jordan - Transformational Mindset and Business Coach and mentor

Why: When I found myself on my own after 31 years of marriage, confused and alone there was a whisper within that told me there was more to my life .... To ignite within myself the capacity to live purposefully , I had to tune into that cry from within and push though the clutter and noise of my fears, uncertainty and determine to rebuild my life and learn to be able to trust myself again.

Facing uncertainty with courage and showing up and saying "Yes" has helped me grow and enlarge my comfort zone and self-belief... There are so many times I was held back by doubt and my own strategies of self-sabotage..

I knew in my 50's, that if I was to transform my life I had to get on with it.., time is a precious commodity so I pledged to take opportunities that aligned with my values and "say Yes " and as I show up I work it out along the way....

As I have committed to this habit, I have had so many new and amazing experiences and also lived some of my bucket list experiences.. , which has been so beautifully healing for me.

In the journey of embracing this habit despite my fears of " I am not enough" , my self trust has grown and I have become a different woman to the woman who started out on this journey to reclaim and rebuild her life....To reclaim the gift of freedom from my past conditioning and embrace the magnificence of my own sense, of who I am and to own my truth is empowering.

This entrepreneurial journey is full of uncertainty and choices that only I can make ..If I waited until I was comfortable and felt equipped with a sense of certainty I would still be waiting at the starting blocks..

I am learning to have a better relationship with uncertainty and the unknown, my scope of influence increases my ability to be more flexible and not have all the answers , this becomes a strength within you.

Coming to a place where I am more comfortable with

imperfect action, and even failing has been liberating as it is in the failing that I have learnt so much about myself and at times had to dig deeply to pick myself up find my passion , self-trust and forge forward .

That moment I said Yes to me, meant I was greater than my circumstances and so began the journey of tapping into and reclaiming the unique qualities that had been buried through the journey of life ,taking on those roles of people pleaser , hero, and rescuer, all to fit in, find that sense of belonging and sense of worthiness. My emotions were often buried in my responsibility of raising a large family and not having healthy boundaries. so to be able to be spontaneous, curious, playful and find that sense of fearlessness has been a beautiful journey back to me... and that one habit of saying "Yes " and working out how has served me well. Each day is a choice to embrace all life has for me as I continue to Reclaim, Rebuild and Radiate my truth, purpose and passion to the world...and help other women to do the same.

The Un-Habit: Waiting for all your ducks to ling up before you are ready to step out and take that 1st step or to say yes to an opportunity

Why: If you wait for all your ducks to be lined up you will miss opportunities, you will still be standing at the starting line waiting, procrastinating and feeling stuck..., all the while others have just got on with it and been prepared to take imperfect action.

Being willing to not get it all right, being ok with failing forward changes everything as the fear of failure so often keeps us stuck in the waiting.

It is in the stepping out into the unknown that courage shows up for you.. Once you have that courage you are open to many possibilities and opportunities... One thing I have learnt from various mentors is ... they all feel fear or a sense of anxiety at times. The difference is they say YES and take that imperfect action to show up and let the magic happen.

Have you ever thought that you could have done something better than what someone else has done ? I have and then realized that I wasn't the person in the arena. I was the one standing on the side lines.

When you step out and take imperfect action you are learning and growing from the experiences, from the successes and the failures. Often the failures can be more valuable than the successes in terms of growth and clarity.

Life is about showing up and experiencing your best life and becoming the best version of yourself so you can live an awesome life... One think I know as I approach 60 , is that the clock is ticking and this life is not a dress rehearsal, have you noticed how fast the years are flying.?

Take that step into the swift waters and trust you can swim, you will soon learn how. ☺

Stack evidence on the side that says " Take massive action towards your goals. The time is now.

Feel the liberation when you allow yourself to take that 1st step of imperfect action ... and see what transforms.

 **About** Robyn: Robyn Jordan is a Transformational mindset coach and mentor. Robyn helps middle aged woman reclaim, rebuild and radiate their truth after losing her own identify in the process of raising and home educating her 7 children, moving countries and experiencing many unfulfilled dreams and disappointments.

She is a breast cancer thriver 2011 she was diagnosed, and she has been on a quest ever since to reclaim and rebuild her life after going through depression and an emotionally destructive marriage

Finding herself on her own after her 31 year marriage broke down, she found herself homeless, financially ruined and experiencing a sense of brokenness and shame. Being a woman of faith meant she had to navigate the roads of letting her marriage go, which was against everything she had believed...

In 2016 she said YES to herself when attending a seminar called "Courage to be You" One of the trainers said " self belief was not required" and the gates were opened to those deep desires of the pathway she wanted to pursue. The desire to be all she was destined to be , her passion to create change and to help others would be what propelled her forward and the how would reveal itself along the journey... Robyn is a certified master practitioner life and business coach and a certified practitioner of meta dynamics. She has a growth mindset and a lover of life...

Her speciality is the journey within, where she help woman answer that whisper within that there is more, more to them and more to life...

To reclaim and rebuild that inner core as she guides woman through the chipping away at the crud and crust of decades of conditioning and limiting beliefs to discover their authentic self within. To remove the false roles we take on in life, so often to protect ourselves ,like people pleaser, hero, rescuer and remove the masks and un-enmesh from those tribal cycles that have kept them living life taking on a false sense of responsibility for the lives of others and often the happiness of others...

Robyn helps woman live consciously, learning to nurture and practice self-care , which is so often neglected in the pursuit of taking care of others...

To reclaim a healthy self-esteem with healthy boundaries, emotions that are able to be expressed resourcefully and to be able to communicate their needs to develop rich relationships with others... remembering the most important relationship begins with you.

Robyn takes her clients on a journey home, to living their truth and authenticity while embracing their vulnerability , passion and purpose....

Robyn's courage to not be defined from her past and her

desire to life an extraordinary life despite the setbacks and heartaches of life inspires others to discover what is innately within them to live their dreams and become woman their future selves can be proud of ...Take that 1st step to say YES and work out how along the way...

To to able to live life with joy and purpose is a gift Robyn has to share with others... To dare to dream of what is possible and marvel at who she has become along the way ... Her motto is as a 58 year old woman is "It is never too late" If not now .... When ?

It is your time to shine.

8

THE HABIT: SPEAK YOUR TRUTH, EVEN IF YOUR VOICE SHAKES - SHEREE TRASK

The Habit: Speak Your Truth, Even If Your Voice Shakes

By Sheree Trask - Writer, Speaker, Rebel, Thought-Leader

Why: For far too long, we've allowed our light to be dimmed by gender roles, fear of rejection or judgment, lack of confidence that we can make a difference, or simply our inability to recognize our unique worth and enough-ness. That all stops now. Because of you - all of us! - are capable and more than we could imagine.

It's time to stop being SILENT. It's time to speak the truth you feel trembling deep within your soul. It's time to shift your internal dialogue to create something more aligned to the essence that is you. It's time to connect and reclaim your power because women, I see you. And your light is begging to be set free.

As women, we've shut down. We've made silent and afraid of our normal. We've allowed societal expectations to cloud the truth that we are fierce and free and fundamentally necessary to creating a greater oneness for humanity and everything beyond. This doesn't serve you, and it certainly doesn't serve the world.

Women. The most sacred creation on the planet. The bringers of life. The nurturers. The mothers. The divine manifestation of feminine grace, softness, beauty, sensuality, and desire. Who we are and what we have to offer matters. Our contribution is imperative for us all to evolve and expand the container here on Earth.

Silent no more, my sisters. Together we fall, together we rise. This is a new era for our spirits to soar. Along in sisterhood, we are guiding one another towards the ultimate truth - love. For ourselves, for humanity, for the world as a whole as we show up in our perfectly imperfect mess. It is not your job to conform to make others comfortable. If you want to create change, sometimes that means you have to shake shit up. And always, it will take courage.

But you're courageous! And what you have to say matters. So when you question your worth or your purpose on this planet, know that there is a reason you were given a voice. There is a reason you were given free will and thought and every experience you've encountered. And it's time to harness that melodious voice of yours and use it to help elevate humanity. It starts with you.

When you choose to lean into the fear and do it anyway, you permit others to do the same. You inspire and empower a new generation of leaders... we need you!

So even when it feels scary... speak. Let your voice tremble. Let your heart flutter. Let your palms sweat. Let the tears fall softly down your cheeks. But speak, because you matter, and your voice will move mountains that others will someday be brave enough to climb. Let's show all the girls and women that are too scared to be seen what's possible when we lean in and share our hearts.

Because when you show up, you light the path for others to walk and find their way home. Together, sweet soul, we can change the world.

The Un-Habit: Ignoring the Nudges

Why: You know those little voices or feelings you get in your tummy, or maybe even your heart? You're not crazy! These divine nudges are trying to tell you something. Think of these 'hits' like a baby that can't quite speak yet.

The baby stirs... then begins to whine... then, after trying to get your attention, they go into a full-blown meltdown, begging for your attention in the only way they know-how.

Our nudges are like that. Often they begin quietly. We don't pay much attention, and gradually, they become louder, stronger. And then, BAM! Full. On. Adult. Melt-down. And we think, "How the hell did this happen? I didn't see this coming!" But I'm willing to bet that if you took the time to tune in and create the awareness available to you, you'd find that your nudges have been lovingly showing up over and over again, trying to get your attention, and only getting louder the longer you chose to ignore them.

Think of your relationships, or jobs, or even places you've lived. The ones that didn't work out probably came with some warning signs, no? In my experience, it's the rebellious side of our spirits that chooses to see what happens if we go about our lives on our terms.

That's the funny thing about free will. Sure, we can do whatever we feel like. But that doesn't mean it's always the best decision, and one that will support our highest good.

When you begin to listen and honor without questioning and needing to know why, or how... you'll find that things start to flow more efficiently, and all that unnecessary stress begins to dissipate. Being tapped into our inner knowing is such a gift and one that takes practice. If you are facing something now that feels unsettling, take a moment to sit with yourself in silence. And remember that nothing outside of you can create the feeling within you. You are in charge of your thoughts, which create your emotions, which lead to actions, which create your reality.

Those nudges are not by accident. Are you willing to

surrender and trust that all will unfold as it should when you give up the need to control and allow your inner voice to take flight?

About Sheree: Sheree Trask is a Content Creator & Consultant, International Empowerment Speaker, and seasoned Ghostwriter. She works with entrepreneurs and conscious brands to bring their vision to voice through collaborative writing in an effort to empower the world.

She's also Certified as a Yoga Instructor and Holistic Health Coach (non-practicing), and carries a fierce determination to create space for everyone to be truly seen and heard, as they are. She's spent 15+ years studying the mind-body connection and empowering women to feel safe in their body's.

With a knack for words, a passion for empowering others to take ownership of their lives and a strong belief in personal growth and exploration, Sheree is on a mission to help transform the hearts and minds of humanity so that together, we can raise the collective consciousness of our world and truly be free to live unapologetically out loud.

She is currently writing her first book, What Was It For?, to be released in 2020.

9

FEARLESSLY LIVE OUT LOUD AS YOUR BEST SELF EACH DAY - KRYSTYLLE RICHARDSON

The Habit: Fearlessly Live Out Loud as your BEST SELF Each Day

By Krystylle Richardson - Leadership & Mindset Expert, International Best Selling Author, Radio Show Host, Red Carpet Interviewer, Missionary

Why: This is an essential habit because so many are living life daily, with a bucket over their fantastic talents and a hood on their creative thoughts just to fit in. That was once me as a child and even into adulthood. Caring what others thought was the norm. It also overshadowed the positivity being spoken into my life. It should have been the other way around where I listened more to the right things. I have found that this habit has catapulted me into the beautiful world of self-acceptance, freedom, and power. I found that the moment that I said to myself that I would not dim my light for anyone, that was the day that I was released from my mental prison of low self-esteem.

I now realize that I cannot dwell on my past of being bullied anymore and cannot surrender any more precious minutes of my life. Being a woman action taker in this sense means taking action to have daily MINDSET SHIFTS. One study showed that 75% of girls with low self-esteem reported engaging in harmful activities when feeling poorly about themselves. I say no more. Any time you feel yourself settling back into negative thoughts and self-limiting behaviors, use this habit. Even go as far as to say the words MINDSET SHIFT, then speak those words that build you up that only you know. This is a habit that helps YOU to stand up for YOU. A habit of living out loud shuts out the noise. Then, you can focus on only letting in the things that accelerate your actions to be your BEST SELF continuously. No facebook likes or Instagram comments can give you that. This is just you living life fearless, free, and with faith in yourself. Not afraid of being the bold and bodacious you that you were meant to be. Being accepting of constructive criticism when appropriate from real mentors but not from the peanut gallery is okay. Living life in this manner raises your frequency to a point where people can help but see your brilliance, love, and unique genius. Please implement this MINDSET SHIFT throughout each day by fearlessly live out loud starting now. This habit WILL change your life. It has transformed mine. I am thankful to God for shifting my thinking and helping me to love being ME bodaciously.

The Un-Habit: The habit of complacency

Why: Complacency is the opposite of impact in my mind. I have been there more times than I wish to admit. Have you as well? People know me as a go-getter, genuine lover of life, and a person that gets things done. Being honest, sometimes, I don't want to be bothered. That thought lasts maybe 10 seconds, though, and I am pressing forward once again. I have to. We have to. There is so much opportunity, especially in our current day and age. So much that could be created improved and enjoyed. So much money to be made, so much love to be shared, and so many people that could be helped. Who has time to be complacent? The more we can take responsibility for ourselves and take action on the things that matter, the more impact we would have. The bible says in James 1:22 to be doers of the word and not hearers only. This is the same for us with all of the seminars, books, tv, and mentor time we pay for. Being overly content with just hearing might be the death of many dreams and inventions that were meant to be manifested to help someone. I challenge you the same as I challenge myself. Take action on your dreams.

Don't let complacency rob the world of what you have to offer. Do what you were placed on this earth to do. No more complacency. Rest when needed. Then, let us get back to work together and let us leave this world better than when we arrived in it. My goal is never to wake up, wondering what if. So do you have this complacency habit? I hope this little note has urged you to un-habit it, once and for all. Fingers crossed.

ABOUT KRYSTYLLE: Krystylle is known in various circles as "The Leadership Expert". As an International Speaker-International Best-Selling Author-Radio Show Host-Red Carpet Interviewer- Missionary, she is hyper-focused on IMPACT! Krystylle has spoken and trained on leadership, mindset and business in conferences and missions all across the U.S. as well as in 25 countries. Her radio show Soaring With Eagles has reached over 35 countries and counting. Krystylle is growing a reputation as The Mindset Mentor. Krystylle uses her 40+ years of global industry and entrepreneur experience to accelerate the Dreams to Destiny cycle for her clients as they find their "Leader Within." She is now transforming her years of leadership/mindset//business training and speeches into paperback books and online media for global distribution. A victim of bullying, Krystylle uses her influence to motivate others to focus on kindness as a way of everyday life. With kindness and give back models infused into her training and keynotes, she has influenced positive change in profits and self-worth on an international level for big corporations, small businesses, churches, families and individuals. Krystylle's new show Above Your Best, focuses on Lifestyle, Leadership and Legacy. The mission of this show is to FOCUS her listeners on really digging deep, past all mindset myths, rising to their full potential based on MINDSET ACTIONS for every season. Once you have reached your best in one season, you will have learned so much that you will have a new best to aspire to in no time. Krystylle believes that complacency is the killer of dreams and it is her desire to see everyone rise from dreams to destiny. Her motto that she has audiences chanting at the top of their lungs is "NEVER settle for less, BE ABOVE Your Best!" Feel free to take this as your own and chant it every day. It does the mind good.

10

DEVELOP THE CLARITY OF 'WHAT DO I WANT?' - SARA ENGLISH

The Habit: Develop the clarity of 'What do I want?'

By Sara English - International Coach, Trainer and Speaker with Master Results

Why: In life, we get what we focus on. When most people are asked what they want, they often list all the things they don't want in their lives. When challenged, very few can state precisely what they DO want in their lives. What we focus on is where our energy lies, and our mind is designed to show us what we pay attention to in our thoughts into the greater world around us. Ever notice how you become interested in something, or it becomes of value in your life, and then you see it everywhere. For example, if wanting to become pregnant or are pregnant, you seem to notice every pregnant person around. Or you buy a new car and then see that car everywhere, whereas you had never really seen it beforehand. This isn't just a phenomenon we experience; it's a real thing. It's called our "Reticular Activating System" (RAS). Do's and don'ts don't govern the system; it is purely what we pay attention to. Therefore, if we are focusing on what we don't want, then our mind will filter the world around us to show us how 'that' presents in our world. This can become compounding as the more we then see it, and the more attention we pay to it, the more our mind shows us more. If we can't identify precisely what we DO want, how can we ever get there? Or how do you know you don't already have it.

So as a habit, the question is to ask ourselves specifically, 'What do I want?'. Not what others want for you, or you think others think you should do, but what exactly DO YOU want in your life. Ideally, it is to ask yourself in all areas of your life: Personal, Career, Family, Friendships, and Relationship, and to write it all down for yourself. When we write things down, they become real.

For many women, what do I want for me, and me only can be a hard question as most are used to fulfilling the needs of others. However, if you think of yourself as a battery, what you want for you, what satisfies you, recharges your battery. The fuller your battery, the more you have to offer those around you. Your response can be big items like your personal goals (i.e., traveling to particular destinations, having individual experiences, learning a language, etc.), all the way down to daily or weekly activities, hobbies or behaviors that are fulfilling to you and create satisfaction and achievement (I.e., exercise, walking the dog, having a long soak bath, having a massage, or reading a book). You are your greatest resource, and if you do not know how to take care of yourself and recharge your batteries on a daily and weekly basis, then you are preventing yourself from being the best version of you.

This is not a question that you ask once and are done. It is a question that requires review and updating as life changes and our priorities change. Therefore it may take you a couple of weeks to do initially and then is reviewed at least monthly to ensure you are keeping on track to your goals and staying in the drivers' seat of your life. Whatever you write down is correct as long as it is what you want, and not for others. We are only genuinely driven by things we want for ourselves.

The Un-Habit: Limit technology, especially email and social media for the first 2 hours of your day at home and 1 hour of your work day.

Why: Technology has entered our lives at superspeed. If we reflect over the last 5, 10, 15, 20 years, most of our lives have changed dramatically due to technology. And while this technology has assisted in so many areas of life, it is easy to get caught up by the technology and become reactive rather than proactive in our day.

The easiest way to become reactive is responding to information rather than planning our day and taking action on it. Email and social media distract us from our intentions, and very quickly, we find that we are reacting to the social media posts, comments, messages, which is known to affect our mood based on what we see. Or reviewing emails and either taking action from them or replying, which has distracted us from a proactive action step within their own lives.

So many people say they have checked their phones, social media, and emails before even getting out of the bed in a morning. That means before they have yet gotten out of bed, they are reactive to other people's words, requests, and demands. This information is then consuming their thoughts and focus. Therefore the habit to break is to remove those behaviors from the first couple hours of your day.

In the first couple of hours of the day, our minds are the most focused and energized. Use this time to be proactive, set your intention, and take one step/action towards your goal. After that time, you can become reactive to your day via technology. In that hour, you will achieve another step towards your goals as an action taker, and this will, in turn, lead to increased motivation and satisfaction in your journey.

Results are what matter in life. Effects of creating the balance you want in your life. Results of creating your purpose. Results of creating your results both personally and professionally. By removing the habit of technology via social media and email first up in the morning, you are keeping focused on the things that matter in your life.

ABOUT SARA: Sara English is passionate about empowering people to gain clarity and direction in their lives, and utmost, take action to create results. Sara started her career in not-for-profit organizations assisting people to overcome personal challenges, moving to establish TFD Services in 2008 and Master Results in 2013 which has assisted thousands of people to overcome both personal and professional hurdles preventing success in their lives. With a background in psychology and business, by mastering one's mind, success can be created in all areas of life. Sara now works between Australia and New Zealand with both individuals, couples, business owners, to address their barriers to success through individual coaching, training and workshops, and speaking roles. Sara's motto in life is that the only limitation in life is the one we place on ourselves. Remove the limitations and create unbounded success. Action is the key to results.

11

PRACTICE ACTIVE LISTENING - DIANA PARRA

The Habit: Practice Active Listening

By Diana Parra, M.A. - CEO & Founder at Diana Parra International

Why: Have you ever had a conversation with someone where you walked away feeling heard and understood even if you didn't agree on the topic and had completely different points of view? It is entirely possible to have this type of communication, but this requires that you practice active listening. You see, we all seek to be seen, heard, and understood.

The problem is that most people "hear" what the other person is saying, but they don't really "listen." We get caught up in thinking how to respond or defend our point, which distracts us from truly listening and understanding what the other person is saying. Active listening enables us to form meaningful relationships and connections. It builds trust and cohesion. We can make active listening a habit if we practice it over time.

So what exactly is active listening? There are three critical elements to active listening: attention, feedback, and response.

Attention includes making and maintaining eye contact, putting away all distractions such as phones and computers, and focusing on the here and now of the conversation. You want to listen to everything the other person has to say first before thinking about what you are going to say next and how you are going to respond. This way, you avoid being distracted from what the other person is saying. Often, we focus so much on how we are going to react that we stop listening to what the other person is saying. This is one sure way to break down communication. Try your best not to interrupt. Interrupting can frustrate the other person, and the message might not be fully understood. Instead, allow the speaker to finish each point before asking questions and don't interrupt with counterpoints as this might put them on the defensive.

Provide feedback by asking questions for clarification, such as "What do you mean?" "Is this what you mean?" or "Can you tell me more?" You can also paraphrase to reflect that you are listening by using statements such as "What I hear you saying is..." or "It sounds like you are saying ..."

Finally, your response needs to be transparent and honest. Be respectful and treat the other person with understanding and kindness. Remember that you can be assertive without attacking the other person or putting down their point of view. Their point of view is valid.

One of my clients was the CEO of a small company. He was very driven and motivated. He was also very logical in his approach to things. His team had a difficult time relating and communicating with him. The feedback revealed that they felt he didn't care about them and was only focused on "getting things done." They also thought that he didn't listen to them, seemed distracted, and was always in a rush to go do "something more important".

Once he understood what active listening is, he realized how his team could perceive his "let's get it done" approach as somewhat dismissive. Through coaching, he learned that it was his responsibility to manage the perception others had of him if he wanted his team to trust him and perform better. Active listening changed the way he was perceived, and ultimately his team developed more trust and respect for him, leading to higher performance and more job satisfaction on both sides.

When you practice active listening, you can stay focused on the other person, truly listen and understand their point of view. You are then more likely to engage in a mutually respectful way, hear their point of view, and have yours heard as well. You do not need to agree with them, but you do need to respect their opinion. Making

active listening a habit will change all of your relationships.

The Un-Habit: Spending too much time on Social Media

Why: A couple of years ago, I worked with a client who told me she was always stressed because she didn't have enough time to accomplish her daily goals both in her business and her personal life. I suggested she keep track of how she was spending her time for a week. She was shocked to find out how much time she was spending on social media. Armed with this knowledge, she decided to limit her daily time spent on social media and to use that time purposefully. She became intentional about how she used social media, and by doing that, she found more time to work on her goals. This was a game-changer for her.

Social Media is a beautiful way to stay connected with friends and family. You can also meet like-minded indi-
viduals through groups, and it can be used to promote your brand and business. However, we often spend too much time scrolling through the endless newsfeeds and posts without a particular goal in mind, and we can easily get lost in it for hours. Decide you will use social media with a goal in mind. That goal can be to connect with a friend or family member, to add value and learn something in a group or to promote your business/brand by adding value to your tribe.

By being intentional about how you use it, you can gain

more time to do other things. You can spend that newly found time going for a walk, spending time with loved ones, practicing self-care, cooking a healthy meal, or working on that business deadline. The possibilities are endless. The point is for you to control how you spend your time on social media, not the other way around. You will feel less stressed, and your relationships will improve.

About Diana: Diana Parra, M.A. is a leadership coach and transformational strategist for female entrepreneurs and professional women, a high performance coach for female executives, a speaker, and an author.

She is the founder and CEO of Diana Parra International and Akros Leadership International. Akros is a leadership development company whose mission is to create a community of leaders dedicated to empowering and inspiring others by leading with love and compassion, while elevating the world at large.

Her 20 plus years of combined experience as a manager, therapist, coach, and consultant have forged in her a unique approach to leadership development. She holds a Bachelor's degree in Psychology from Rutgers University and a Master's degree in Educational Psychology with a concentration in Clinical Psychology from Montclair State University. Diana has also completed doctoral level coursework in Organizational Psychology at the Rutgers University Graduate School of Applied and Professional Psychology and is a graduate of Anthony Robbins Business Mastery and Anthony Robbins Mastery University.

Diana is coauthor of Get It Done: Design the Business of Your Dreams, Get it Designed! Build the Business of Your Dreams and has recently published her own book: Leading with a Broken Heart: Finding Gold in Our Darkest Moments.

Diana was born in Colombia and is bilingual and bi-cultural. She is married with three adoptive children. She loves to explore the world, personal-development, music, yoga, and nature.

12

DO AN ALIGNMENT CHECK-IN WEEKLY, OR DAILY IF POSSIBLE - JENNIFER HARRIS

The Habit: Do an alignment check-in weekly, or daily if possible.

By Jennifer Harris - Founder & CMO, Brand Builder Rethink Ltd. and BrandInk Agency Ltd.

Why: Have you ever heard the quote, "Ask, and you shall receive?" It has a different meaning for different people. However, if you have ever tried to actualize your big goals, then you know that understanding what you are going after is critically important, as is the why. You must make sure to have absolute crystal clarity on this before you start the journey to the ASK.

Sounds simple right?

Well, often, many people struggle with starting this

process. And... they can also struggle at multiple points in the process. But here's the thing, usually, people think because they have a clear vision of what they want, it will simply come to fruition, and that is simply not the case. Many pieces need to come together. And while the why is critically important, it goes beyond just knowing the WHY. While there are many factors, and there is a Blueprint to follow, there is a critical piece that many people don't talk about. You see, a few years ago, I discovered this little nugget and made it into a Habit, which has served me well. And so, I will share it with you today.

Being a strategic marketer, I know how critical it is to strategically plan on your business and the importance of clarity of the WHY. I have been strategic business and marketing planning my whole career as a marketer on National and Fortune 500 brands, as well as entrepreneurs and Small & Medium (SMB) businesses. And this strategic understanding is a critical piece of any strong brand, what we call "Brand Ink," and a key reason we included as part of the Entrepreneurs' Mastery Bootcamp™ within the 7-Step Blueprint ProSeries Sales Igniter™ training program we offer our clients. But this piece, the one not many people talk about, is different... and for me, it became clear that it is needed to be a successful entrepreneur. So much so, that I created a whole separate program around it.

But truthfully, I wish I had known over 15+ years ago what I know now. But, here is the truth... when you are on your true path in entrepreneurship, there is another deeper level unlock that must happen. An unlock that we talk about in one of the Entrepreneurs Mastery Bootcamp ProSeries programs, we call SoulFit Leadership™. This Habit is part of one of the seven keystones to Purposeful Leadership: SoulFit Leadership™ of your life and your business. And that keystone is alignment.

Be in alignment with the Self. Be in alignment with a Higher Good.

Here is the thing. We are all human. There will always be days we are not showing up as our best selves. But when you get clear on this one piece, the rest takes shape for you in a very different way. When you are not in alignment, you are missing that one big piece of the unlock. CONGRUENCY.

Today, often, when I am working with Entrepreneurs, SMBs, and coaches, one can see when INCONCRUENCY challenges clients… when they are not in alignment. This is why I feel our SoulFit Leadership™ Program is such a great unlock for people who are struggling with this and why we encourage all our Entrepreneurs' Mastery Bootcamp ProSeries participants and Alumni to enroll.

So… how do you know if you are incongruent with your ASK on your 'yellow brick road' journey? Well… just ask yourself. Look within first and then look outward. Are you in alignment with your ASK? Is what you see in alignment with Self and a Higher Purpose on your journey to actualize the ASK? If you are, then amazing… you have achieved an unlock that many have yet to discover. But for those of you who are unsure, or said an honest… "you know what… no… ". Then start here.

Get clear on the ASK. And then once you have the ASK, think about it daily. Visualize it. Feel the emotions around achieving the ASK. But then there is the other part of the equation...

To accomplish the ASK to its fullest capacity, you must not only be clear on the ASK on what you want to receive, but then also check-in regularly to see if your actions, and thoughts & emotional expressions are congruent with the ASK. If you are not congruent, simple laws of attraction will not allow you to receive. And that is why alignment is one of the seven keystones to SoulFit Leadership™

Why?

Because you are not 100% in alignment, you are not demonstrating that you are ready for that next level... and so you aren't prepared.

So... Learn the Lesson. Be in Alignment. Be Congruent. And Receive the ASK.

Making this simple Habit of embracing one of the Keystones to SoulFit Leadership™ with a weekly (or daily) alignment check-in helps to course correct you more quickly when you are not "showing-up" to yourself and others as aligned with your goals and achieving your purpose(s) of the ASK.

I hope this Habit brings about a Mindset Rethink™ light bulb... and perhaps we will see you inside the Bootcamp ProSeries Sales Igniter to help with clarity around your why and driving sales growth, and start that SoulFit Leadership™ journey.

The Un-Habit: Stop hiding in your business... So you can start driving your business.

Why: As entrepreneurs, often people think we need to wear all hats. Or least at the start... right? But here is the thing... that is not the case. I would even go as far as to say that it is precisely what you should not be doing, especially in today's gig economy.

How so, you ask? Well, today, now more than ever before, there are a ton of resources entrepreneurs have access to. Resources that are also now, more than ever before, cost-effective. Here is an example of an all too common conversation.

New client: I think I may be finally ready to hire an agency... but I am only 1-person and like doing social media myself... so still not sure.

Me: Let me ask you this. How many hours a week do you spend thinking about the social posts, researching the content, writing the content, developing the creative, scheduling into the planner, etc

New client: A few hours.

Me: So it is fair to say 2 hrs a week, meaning 8 hours a month... give or take?" Then I asked, "What is your hourly rate as a coach?

New client: $300/hr billable rate

Me: Does this include your "social" broadcasts and other publishing activities?

New client: No... then it would be more like 4 hours a week.

Me: Well, let's evaluate this. You are spending about 7-8hrs on just standard content posting a month outside of 'in-person' broadcasts, which at $300/hr for 8 hours is $2400 worth of time. And so, it is fair to say that if you found someone like us that could do it for a fraction of that cost, you would be further ahead already? Plus, if you repurpose that time on revenue-generating activities, or working on strategic plans that are business building, you would be even further ahead. By not work in the business, and repurposing your time, you are driving your business by hiring an expert resource.

Client: I have never actually looked at it this way.

Sounds familiar, right?

Now, why do we do this? Because it is easier to focus on what we know, comfortable with, and what we like to do. But amazing brands with strong business results are not built on staying focused in the weeds. Instead, they focus on driving forward their strategic vision and activating the plan to achieve it. And to do this, you need to prioritize the strategic direction and growth of the company even if you are a 1-person company. The smaller the company, the bigger the impact because you are only 1-

person. Imagine the world where you repurposed that time and took a program like the Entrepreneurs' Mastery Bootcamp to learn some of this business and marketing mastery to drive your business with greater clarity. The time savings alone would more than pay for the program!

Instill this Habit. Ask yourself, does this task drive the business forward? Reprioritize where you focus so that you can shift your efforts onto bigger priorities that will drive your goals forward. Stop trying to do everything.

Create an A-team of partners to surround you and delegate as much as you can. Run the numbers to assess what makes more sense for each task. And remember, if you are working in the business, you are not working at driving the business to its next level.

Try this Exercise Habit over the next three days. Capture all your tasks and then decide what you must do or what can be done for you. If you are like many entrepreneurs, you will realize that a lot could be done by your VAs, agencies, partners, or 3rd party tools and the team, which will then free you up to focus on business growth and building an amazing brand.

ABOUT JENNIFER: Jennifer Harris is a serial entrepreneur, a Business & Marketing Mastery expert, and Performance & Marketing Consultant. Jennifer has been awarded & given recognition by Global and Fortune 500 Brand Leaders on World renown brands for Brand Leadership, Driving Sales Growth, High Performance and more.

Today in her consultancy agency, Founder & CMO of Brand Builder Rethink Ltd, Jennifer embraces SoulFit Leadership in her businesses. Jennifer leverages her over 15 + years of marketing & advertising experience to help Entrepreneurs, Coaches, and Small & Medium-Sized Businesses (SMBs) find their growth path with innovative Entrepreneurs' Mastery Bootcamp™ ProSeries training programs. These programs include the ProSeries Sales Igniter™, Mindset Jumpstart™, Mindset Rethink™, and SoulFit Leadership™ programs.

Jennifer is also Founder & CMO of BrandInk Agency Ltd that offers affordable solutions for Online Digital Services, PR Brand Ink exposure, Social Media, Sales Lead Funnels, and other Brand Ink growth services for Entrepreneur, SMBs, and Coaches who are trying breakthrough, build their brand and grow sales in a highly competitive marketplace.

Jennifer's other key accomplishments include being shortlist as a Top 50 Selects Knowledge Broker speaker of 600 applicants. She most recently launched her Biz Rethink™ Interview Series and launched her new SoulFit Leadership™ Program as a Featured Speaker at an inspiring JSY event. And she is currently working on launching her upcoming book release in late Spring 2020.

In addition to being a serial entrepreneur, is a passionate Feature-Film Screenwriter and she has helped Co-Produce several films, has hosted a TV series segment. She is also an avid Global traveler of over 25+ countries and counting.

We think you will love her Brand Ink!

13

LIVE A LIFE OF EFFICIENCY - MARILEN CRUMP

The Habit: Live a life of Efficiency

By Marilen Crump - Creator of the D.R.E.A.M. Success Strategy and Founder of the Female Income Academy

Why: If you ask me, the best Habit to have is Efficiency!

The hustle, the grind, the sweat, the tears... what if some of these instances were avoidable when it comes to achieving success?

In my experience, when you are trying to do things without working on your efficiencies first, it usually results in you spending more effort than what that task was worth.

There is the adage that you should 'WORK SMARTER,

NOT HARDER,' but people don't always explain how this statement can be performed. I hope that I can give you some enlightenment through the subject of efficiency.

The first step in this process is that you have to know the direction in which you are heading with any task, goal, or desire. This is a MUST. Then you are going to have to unload some stuff - what I call relinquishing - so you can think better. Relinquish fear, hesitation, time clutter, distractions, etc.... YES! When you do this, you're lighter and freer. That is when you can start to create a better plan in a better mode.

As you cultivate the Habit of efficiency, you will need to exercise your vision. Try to imagine things before they happen that you would like to happen. This is a fun and NO COST way to act it all out in your mind before any physical activity. I love that this exercise doesn't result in time lost, money spent, and energy wasted.

The difference for some people is that they are stuck in strictly ACTION mode. They never take the time to become more efficient. They are busy doing things to be busy, thinking, "as long as I'm doing something, I'm getting somewhere" - when, in fact, they are far from it. I can see the stress and aggravation reaching the busy types. They sometimes drift from their direction that they don't even know if what they are doing is going to yield the right results! I espouse being more deliberate in my actions steps. It leads to better success and less stress! I would rather you not work against yourself as well. Let's figure things out and assess the needs before working on it.

Now that you are working along with Efficient ACTION, this phase is active yet filled with a more desirable FLOW and energy. You can do the task all day! This leads to the awesome flow of MOMENTUM where things are at that result that you wanted. You can relish in the rewards! You can even leverage stuff for an even bigger reward.

So there you have it... it would be best if you worked on the Habit of efficiency and the steps that come before and after. And wouldn't you know it? That step-by-step plan is spelled out as D.R.E.A.M. = Direction, Relinquish, Efficiency, Action, and Momentum.

Try it out, but remember that it is not DRE-H-AM, that there is no H in DREAM because you don't need to know the "HOWs," that is revealed to you when you trust this process. And be sure to do it in that order and hit on every part. I know that for those of you already living the life that you have dreamed of, you are probably using this Habit of efficiency that I call the D.R.E.A.M. Success Strategy™. If you want to learn more about it, I encourage you to look up #expertdreamcatcher to help you land on my information and other opportunities to gain more positive habits in your life!

The Un-Habit: Getting Stuck in Indecision

Why: Indecision completely gives you permission to lack in confidence, live in fear, and give power over your life to circumstance. When you are indecisive you don't allow your intuition to prevail. You are on a constant frequency of confusion and this will eventually show up as stress. Maybe the fact that you are already stressed is why you create more of it. No matter the cause, it's a terrible habit to have. It will frustrate those around you and they will stop seeing you as a source of any solutions. This can cause strain in your relationships and in your job or business.

The best way to combat this is to make a decision and stand firm in the results. It's the only way to learn and evolve. When we make a mistake, our brain will adjust to figure out a better way so as to not repeat the same action. When we get a win - it is the same thing, only if it was a direct correlation to a firm decision and action. If things were achieved just by chance, the mind has no foundation on how to base its future action. You are then left with guessing at the decision you need to make - at which the results may not be in your favor.

I've had to learn through my mistakes and each time, I have been able to leverage the knowledge I have earned by making the decisions I have made. Remember this... consequences are neither negative nor positive, it is whatever we perceive the following circumstance to be. We can at any point turn a disappointment to a triumph. We are allowed to learn and make new plans. A new decision.

If you need help making a decision, you can certainly ask for it. However, please be careful with who you allow to help you. Is their mindset open to abundant possibilities or do they concern themselves with fear and lack? Be sure before you take any advice. It's not a good situation when the blind is leading the blind. Find someone more enlightened than you and that's a DECISION you will be rewarded for making!

So remember, if you find yourself at a point of decision. Tap into intuition, make a decision and D.R.E.A.M. your way towards success!

 **About Marilen:** Marilen Crump is a thought leader and business coach based in Yorktown, VA where she resides with her husband, Kenneth and their five children. She is the Founder of Female Income Academy™ and Creator of the D.R.E.A.M. Success Strategy™. She is the President of the Peninsula Women's Network based in Hampton Roads, VA which has been in existence for over 40 years. Marilen also wears the hat of public speaker with talks that have been held at NASA, Civitan International and several University campuses. She was blessed to contribute to a book by authors Kathy Flyer and Sue Urda called "The Gifts of Grace and Gratitude" that made it to #1 Amazon Best-Seller. Marilen's mission is to change the world through the contributions that women can be empowered to make when supported and empowered. She is a native of the Philippines and her ultimate vision is to connect women from different countries to help one

another as a fellowship in entrepreneurship. Marilen's skills center around community and innovation where she can be found creating and sharing thoughts and ideas through her multiple online communities. In her free time, Marilen volunteers at her church, spends time in nature, and is always on the lookout for unique adventures that she can have with her wonderful family.

14

DON'T ALLOW YOUR NEGATIVE EMOTIONS TO SABOTAGE YOUR SUCCESS! - COSETTE A. LEARY

The Habit: Don't Allow Your Negative Emotions to Sabotage Your Success!

By Cosette A. Leary - Founder of From Welfare to The White House

Why: Giving into our negative emotions has the far-reaching ability to sabotage our successes while derailing our dreams. We all have an emotional totem pole, and that's not some new freaky virus being announced on the channel 6 evening news, nevertheless, it is note worthy news and most importantly there is a remedy for navigating through our negative emotions. The name of this mysterious antidote is, the art of elimination baby! Now here's the kicker, think about this, what lingering notions make up your discouraging emotional totem pole? I know the main and obvious answer are you ready, weight for it.... STRESS did you guess that one too.

How many times have you heard someone say, "I'm so stressed out?" How many times have you said those wearisome words yourself? Many times, the habitual root cause of our negative outlook is the fact that we are looking up high at our life's ladder (our totem pole) and we see a Woodpecker! Now the question is what to do about the Woodpecker? This is where the art of elimination comes in, of course, life often affords us devastating challenges such as the death of a loved one, a car wreck or two, terminal illness, loss of a job, or perhaps the loss of a home etc.; but far too often we become worry warts and we dream up discouraging scenarios of what if(s) I for one am guilty of practicing this off-putting obsession. Now check this out, the what if syndrome swings both ways. There's the classic what if things don't pan out the way we want them to, or there is the daydreamers delight, what if I win the Lotto.

Let's first deal with the consideration of things not panning out the way we hope for. Life will often send us a telegram which we won't necessarily like all too well. We can expect that every now and then, but how do you handle change? Can you work through the gridlock of your unconstructive feelings held within the elements of the change that the wind just blew in? Remember when I asked you what makes up your emotional totem pole? Do you really need each figure on this lustrous work of your life or dose some of your life's negative emotional artwork need a new coat of paint, or better yet maybe we need to keep that Woodpecker around for a little while longer? What I am getting at is, do you allow your negative emotions such as fear, anger, regret, and envy to sabotage your success by cosigning the proposition that these emotions are the measure of your irrefutable failure and practice of blame shifting?

If your answer is hinging on these discouraging elements, these sentiments must be chopped down and eradicated! Your self worth is worth far too much to spend precious time on unnecessary issues. My council to you is, don't! Now about that Lotto ticket you don't need to gamble on your life anymore. Set down and make a list of what is certain in your life with a shifted focus on boosting your positive emotions such as your passions, your wins both big and small, areas of happiness within your life and what you certainly want to get out of life. Practice redirecting your energy to celebrating your optimistic outlook on life.

Now go over your list, your emotional totem pole is looking more striking, shinier, it appears more structured three cheers for our superhero, the art of elimination! By readjusting your state of mind and taking positive action steps you now have more room to take on your life's ambitions, you will be able to reach your highest mountain top and place your flag at the very top of the mountain happy navigating!

The Un-Habit: Reacting Through Patterns of Negative Self-Talk

Why: Diving into internal pockets of wounding self-judgement only takes away from the power of our positive actions. Many of us indulge in negative self-talk which is a byproduct of discouraging emotions. Often the emotions tide to this habit are fostered within areas of insecurity. This is often a knee jerk reaction to events which make us feel as if we are parachuting without the proper equipment. While for many of us this may be our first go to practice, by taking a step back and reminding ourselves of our why factor we can celebrate the fact that we have an incredible purpose which is fueled by an amazing passion.

Negative self-talk can become a major roadblock to our success similar to its cousin negative emotions, but it doesn't have to be. Looking at our challenges as new opportunities for growth from uncomfortable experiences will allow us to recognize different ways in which we can enhance our impact of service while rebooting our own self-worth. Here are some great questions to consider asking yourself.

- What project can I take on within the next 90 days that will allow my talents to shine?
- How can I boost my confidence more?
- What am I willing to do to reawaken my passion?
- Who do I know that can become my accountability partner?

- Who can I be a mentor to?
- What are three of my most favorite self-care actions?
- Is there a new hobby that I can take up?
- Are there any social/networking groups that I can join?

When we practice keeping our emotions geared to manifesting positive momentum, through reducing negative self-talk we enhance our areas of continued success and build bridges of opportunity. We must remember that we deserve and are worth the amazing success that our life can bring to us every day!

About Cosette: Cosette "CoCo" Leary loves to live out loud! She is a jubilant Motivational Speaker, Professional Coach, Author, and Educator who has overcome a childhood of poverty, abuse, growing up in orphanages, group homes, and foster homes since the tender age of 12, and finding herself pregnant with her first child at 14 years old.

She has raised four children through hard work and painful decisions and has gone from years of surviving off welfare benefits to earning her University Degree in, Public Administration graduating with the highest honor of, Summa Cum Laude while serving as a staff member in both a Senatorial and Congressional office. Ms. Leary pulled herself out of poverty in order to show others how to do the same. She exists in order to breathe life back into impoverished communities, rekindle relationships across economic class lines and empower women.

15

ALWAYS ASSUME THAT THE BUCK STOPS WITH YOU - VICKY BOLADIAN

The Habit: Always Assume That The Buck Stops With You

By Vicky Boladian - Chief Executive Officer of Aerlex Tax Services/Aviation Tax Attorney and Entrepreneur

Why: Having worked for multiple large organizations, I realized that a project can go from hand to hand multiple times and still remain incomplete or incorrect. As a result of my experiences, I learned to establish systems of review where each individual working on the project believes and understands that they are capable of not only completing the project but also doing the job accurately. If every person in the corporation took this final responsibility upon their shoulders, the final product at the end of the process becomes the best possible product that could be delivered. In this way, there are no excuses and no opportunity to place blame on others.

When I evolved into placing this ultimate burden upon myself, even back when I was the lowest rung on the corporate ladder, I was able to quickly excel and accelerate my growth within the organization.

The following are the steps for Assuming That The Buck Stops With You:

(1) Understand the Goal. It is important that you not start a project until you are certain that you have understood what is being asked of you. I have seen a number of people who would take a project, spin their wheels for hours and end up with the wrong outcome. If you take the time to understand the goal from the beginning, it will save everyone a lot of time and money.

(2) Don't Be Afraid To Ask Questions. Believe me, I too was that person a long time ago. Not wanting to appear stupid, people often avoid asking critical questions that would greatly assist them in achieving the success they desire. Do not be afraid to ask questions!

(3) Prepare Assignment In Advance of Deadline. Always make sure you attack a project well in advance of the due date. In this way, you will feel more in control of the outcome.

(4) Review Work Product Carefully. Do not assume that someone else will catch your mistake down the line. Take the time to review your work in great detail.

(5) Take Time Away To See and Think Clearly. Taking a break can be critical for jobs that require a high level of accuracy. So, don't feel guilty for taking a walk in the park, a day at the beach, a family dinner or simply a good night's sleep. You need that time away to be able to clear your head and reenergize your body.

(6) Regroup and Attack Assignment Again. Once you have cleared your head and reenergized your body, go back and look at your work once more. You will find that you will be able to view it from a different perspective, catch mistakes you had not previously noticed and make sure all angles have been covered.

(7) Present Outcome To Colleague or Client. Whether your project was handed to a manager in your organization or the client, present your product confidently. Make sure you understand every aspect of your project so you are ready to answer any question that could be asked.

(8) Obtain Feedback and Learn From Outcome. Whether the feedback is positive or negative, remember that all feedback is a learning experience. Do your best not to make the same mistake twice. By doing so, you will find that you will evolve into a more skilled and efficient person over time.

The Un-Habit: Stop Procrastinating!

Why: Procrastination is one of the significant obstacles to becoming the best version of yourself. Procrastination is defined as the habitual or intentional delay of starting or finishing a task despite knowing it might have negative consequences. We have all been there, and it begins when we are young. Whether it is completing a book review during summer vacation as a child, an essay in college, or a project given to you as an employee, everyone has probably procrastinated multiple times in their life. However, there can be tremendous negative consequences to procrastination, such as getting bad grades, failing to meet client expectations, or getting fired. No one wants to be perceived as being incompetent by one's peers. Ultimately, it could result in losing confidence in oneself.

The following are my tips for avoiding procrastination:

(1) Delegate As Much As You Can. The key is keeping the momentum going. So, when you hand off a project to someone else to complete, you get that ball rolling. It then becomes important to keep the ball rolling. Once the project or draft comes back to you for review, don't let it sit on your desk for too long. Don't be the bottleneck that keeps progress from taking place.

(2) Take The Harder Path. Sometimes when we are presented with two choices, we select the easier path even though we know in our heart that the correct thing to do was to take the harder path. Take the time to consider which path is the best and then move forward to achieve it. Do not fear the more difficult path as it may bring you rewards you never dreamed of.

(3) Go The Extra Mile. Even if your calendar is full and you are already way too busy, if you know that the

outcome of your goal would be better if you took one more step, do one more thing or research one more topic, just do it. Always go the extra mile to receive the full benefit of your endeavors.

(4) Do Whatever It Takes. Whether it is pulling an all-nighter, pushing yourself harder, or making yourself stronger, do whatever it takes to get the job done correctly.

About Vicky: In her 21 years as a practicing attorney, Vicky Boladian has developed a strong expertise in the complex field of tax law. Since 2008, she has utilized this knowledge in guiding Aerlex Tax Services clients through multi-state sales and use tax exemptions, property tax valuations and appeals, federal excise tax audits and federal and state income tax audit representation. During her years at Aerlex, Ms. Boladian has achieved a 100% success rate in securing use tax exemptions and has saved her clients millions of dollars in state and federal tax appeals.

Ms. Boladian has spoken on aviation tax issues to various organizations, including the National Business Aviation Association and Helicopter Association International. She has been selected by Southern California Super Lawyers as one of the top attorneys in the Southern California region from 2014 to 2019, and named to the Top 50

Women Lawyers in that area from 2015 to 2018. She is ranked in Chambers and Partners as one of the top aviation attorneys worldwide from 2017 to 2019.

Prior to becoming the CEO and co-owner of Aerlex Tax Services, Ms. Boladian worked for Arthur Andersen and Ernst & Young. At Andersen, she assisted high net-worth clients on a wide variety of complex tax law issues. At Ernst & Young, she represented corporations, partnerships and individuals in audits by the Internal Revenue Service and the California Franchise Tax Board. Ms. Boladian is also an entrepreneur and a licensed real estate broker who has handled both residential and commercial real estate transactions. A 1997 graduate of the Boston University School of Law, she received her undergraduate degree in political science from the University of California at Irvine in 1994.

16

CHOOSE PROACTIVITY BEFORE REACTIVITY - MACKENZIE WATTS

The Habit: Choose Proactivity Before Reactivity

By Mackenzie Watts - Creator of Mindset by Mackenzie/Anxiety Awareness Advocate & Coach

Why: How much of your day is for you?

For most of us, we are solving other people's problems from the moment we wake up. The first thing we do is grab our phone from the bedside table. We answer texts. We respond to emails. We reply to social media comments.

Our mind is flooded with how we are going to please other people.

"I need to schedule a time to meet my friend for coffee."

"I need to get this report finalized for my boss."

"I need to respond to Aunt Susan's comment."

By doing this, you are choosing to address the concerns of others instead of doing things you want to do for you. The things that would move your life in the direction you want instead of the direction others see for you.

If you spend your life solving other people's problems, you are not living your life.

While it's not realistic to go about your day and not care about meeting your deadline or caring for your family, everyone can find time in the morning to be proactive before reactive.

Every morning I complete my morning routine without checking texts, email, social media, etc. I do this because I know that as soon as I do, my mind will start thinking of what I'm going to respond with, how I need to change my plans for this person and all the problems I need to solve for other people. By having this hour of proactive, not reactive, time to myself each morning, I'm building the life I want to live and not the life others expect me to live.

No matter how many obligations you have, how successful you are, how "needed" you are, everyone can find time in the morning for themselves. Try waking up just 30 mins before you usually do to work on yourself - your friends, family, boss, acquaintances wouldn't expect you to reply during this time anyways.

If you are yearning for a full life where you feel aligned with your true self, where you have discovered your potential and purpose, you are going to have to start by investing in yourself. Not willing to wake up a little earlier or feel like the needs of others are more important than your own? Nothing changes if nothing changes. No one will make your dreams happen for you. You have to get real with yourself and ask if you are willing to sacrifice your life for the wants and needs of others. If the answer is no, start choosing a morning of proactivity before reactivity. You deserve a morning for you because the rest of your day will be for everyone else.

The Un-Habit: Hitting the Snooze Button

Why: I was NEVER a morning person. Sleeping in until 11 a.m. on weekends was to be expected. I would work crazy hours all week and then "catch up" on sleep over the weekend. On weekdays, I would hit snooze over and over until it was 10 minutes before I needed to leave and then be in a panic to get where I needed to be in such a short amount of time.

At some point, I realized this was not a healthy or sustainable structure. I was starting my day anxiety-filled, and it would only get worse from there.

I wanted to wake up earlier and stop hitting that snooze button, but I saw no value in being awake just for the sake of it. Why would I waste my precious sleep only to be awake a little earlier? So, I gave myself a reason to be awake - ME time!

I decided this time would allow me to work on myself

while simultaneously setting myself up for a successful (non-anxiety-filled) day. My me time started with just 10 minutes of gratitude, which eventually evolved into now waking up at 6 a.m. and having 2 hours of "me" time.

To stop hitting snooze, you need to give yourself a good reason to be awake. This time will look different for all of us. Maybe for you, it means having time to work on your dream business. For someone else, it might mean taking their dog for a walk while listening to their favorite podcast. For another, maybe it means getting their workout done in the morning, so they have more time with their family after work.

You won't just magically become a morning person, and to stop hitting the snooze button, you have to take steps that will help get you there. Choose one small thing you want to do and start doing it each morning. Soon the snooze button won't be a problem, and you'll look forward to your precious "me" time each morning.

About Mackenzie: Mackenzie Watts is the creator of Mindset by Mackenzie, an anxiety awareness blog, and coaching brand. Her mission is to let others know they are not alone by sharing her mental health journey and the tools that have helped her overcome overwhelming anxiety and extreme perfectionism.

Mackenzie grew up in a small town in Iowa with a supportive, loving family and community. There she lived a normal childhood, went to college only a few miles from home, and landed great jobs close to home in her preferred field of study. Life was great and was set up exactly how she intended.

Meanwhile, perfectionism was pushing her to be harder on herself than any person deserves, and anxiety was causing overwhelming hurdles each day.

Sleepless nights recalling each conversation she had and what should have been said. She was planning for future problems that would never occur. Overextending herself to try and compensate for what she thought she was unable to provide. Friendships were limited, and there was no desire to meet new people.

One day she realized this was not a sustainable way of living, and some significant changes needed to happen. She began her physical, but more importantly, mental health journey, which has ultimately made her into the exact opposite of the "Old Mackenzie" description above.

Mackenzie now resides in San Diego, California, and commits her life to share her story and what has helped her out of anxiety so others will feel empowered to let go of fear and live into their marvelous potential.

17

FIND A WAY TO FIND THE WAY - SHYLA DAY

The Habit: Find a Way to Find the Way

By Shyla Day - Award Winning Singer, CEO, TED Speaker, Humanitarian

Why: Since I was young, my mother told me we would "find a way to find the way." It took my whole life and ten years in business to understand what exactly she meant finally. "Find a way to find the way" is a habit I developed young, even if I didn't realize it. It is precisely what I've been doing in business and life to become who I am as a woman of action today! You see, I grew up in a single-parent home due to my fathers' early, unexpected death, and we'd have to come up with some incredibly creative solutions to make ends meet.

We'd always start with baby steps. First stop, find a way. Finding "a way" is a simple shift in perspective. If there ever was a problem, there were always a million solutions. Secondly, we would find the way. Finding "the way" is thinking outside of the box. If we had a goal, there were a million pathways to get there. Limitations and circumstances are just the frameworks of how you will get to where you need to go. If you stop to think from a different perspective and then think outside of the box, you are sure to get creative with your solutions and achieve your goals.

For example, if you are an inventor and you have a concept or idea, the next step should be to identify what problems you might have along the way. Knowing which issues you might face means you are just one step closer to bridging that gap between you and your end-goal. The most prolific of inventors were given limitations so unheard of many would have deemed their end-goals impossible; until finally, that lightbulb sparked on (literally and figuratively)! Your most significant limitations, or your circumstances, are simply a rulebook that you get to find the loopholes in to get to your destination. When you find a way to find the way, you are taking the time to think up an adaptive and strategic method of leaping, skipping, crawling, ducking (a million ways, remember?) over that bridge of limits straight into your bliss. Developing this kind of unconventional habit is giving you the upper hand advantage because after all, one well thought out plan is better than ten shots in the dark.

I am not saying this will be easy, but I will say that it is worth it. I challenge you this- get creative and accomplish one thing you've already done before in a brand new way.

The Un-Habit: Inability to accept failure

Why: "Only those who dare to fail can ever achieve greatly." Robert F. Kennedy

It never feels good when something doesn't go as planned. However, failing is an indefinite part of human growth. Understanding that each of us is human, nobody is perfect; we have feelings- we often make mistakes that lead to failure, which makes each of us more powerful in the end! We humans are a sucker for comfort. When put in uncomfortable situations, such as trying something new that can go wrong- can often lead to cold feet. As a result, we end up making the same comfortable decisions and actions we are sure to provide that ease of tension, knowing there isn't even the slightest possibility we can fail. More often than not, when a person has the un-Habit of inability to accept failure, they won't even try to achieve that dream or goal to avoid that shame and guilt we feel if and when we do fail. If you don't try- you can't succeed. Gain a new perspective and change your thought process on what failing means to you. Each misstep is a teachable moment! Choosing to learn, grow, and accept failures does not mean you are proud of or celebrating your faux pas- it's healthier to accept that failure as a fact. It takes a specific mental discipline to "un-Habit" what we've learned about failure over time. Reframe how and what you think and feel about failing.

As long as you view your mistakes as tools for learning, you will be in a better headspace to move forward in your next step towards what might be your greatest success! For every 1000 failures, there is one victory. Thomas Edison once said, "I didn't fail 1,000 times. The light bulb was an invention with 1,000 steps".

I challenge you this- find a decorated person of distinction that you admire who has never failed (not even once).

About Shyla: Shyla Day is a young award-winning singer/songwriter, TED Speaker, and International Humanitarian, who has more accolades than she is years old.

Her personal brand has garnered over 26 award nominations, distribution in 189 countries, and dozens of sponsorships, endorsements, and business partnerships. As an Entrepreneur, Shyla's brand has been recognized for a 2017 Entrepreneur Award and was selected as a Top Nominee in 2018. Shyla Day also received National Recognition as an American Small Business Champion. In 2019 Shyla received the Young Entrepreneur Award at All Women Rock.

As a headliner of Sold Out Shows at legendary venues such as the House of Blues and Whiskey a Go Go, Shyla is not shy to being on the stage. She has performed 2 tours with the "Tunes For Tots" charity foundation, released a live EP and an official single "Kiss Me"- which landed her the Best Onstage Performer nomination at the EZ Way Wall of Fame Awards, 6 consecutive Artists In Music Award Nominations, a Ventura County Award Nomination, 3 Josie Music Award nominations, and 3 Los Angeles Music Award, Pheonix Music Award, Hollywood F.A.M.E Award Nominations.

Seen by millions on radio, TV and Magazines, such as Rolling Stone, Billboard, iHeart Radio, ABC, CBS, and many more Shyla has used her large platform as a public-figure and music artist to support hundreds of charity and non-profit organizations internationally. "Shyla [...] desires to have a positive impact on the global community", honor society President James W. Lewis stated. Examples of supported initiatives include funding a dormitory for girls in Uganda, the clean water initiative, encouraging youth from all over the world to stand up to social issues that are important to them, and so (so) much more! Claes Nobel, of the Nobel Prize Family, stated "Shyla...represents our very best hope for the future".

Shyla led a passionate led talk on the TEDx platform with over 20 million subscribers, called "Music for Global Impact", where she sparks conversation on unconventional humanitarian efforts all over the world.

A proven fan favorite, Shyla Day has been nominated for 4 Fans Choice/Fan Favorite awards (Josie Music Awards, Artists in Music Awards, Ventura County Music Awards, and Los Angeles Music Awards).

Shyla continues to be a role model to young girls all over the world by continuing her education after earning 4 college degrees with honors and pursuing an education at both Yale and at Harvard University for Entrepreneur-ship and Music for Social Action. She is a member of 2 honors societies and has also been given a medal for "Academic Achievement and the Pursuit of Excellence", a national honor by Claes Nobel.

Claes Nobel, of the Nobel Peace Prize Family stated, "I am honored to recognize the hard work, sacrifice, and commitment that Shyla has demonstrated. Shyla is a member of a unique community that represents our very best hope for the future". Being born on Labor day- Shyla Day is living up to the hustle.

18

MODEL THE BEHAVIOR YOU ADMIRE IN OTHERS - NEELU GIBSON

The Habit: Model the behavior you admire in others

By Neelu Gibson - Co-Founder and President, Seaglass RQA LLC.

Why: Modeling the behavior, you admire in others is a lesson I learned from several fantastic leaders over my career. This lesson applies whether you are a business professional at an individual contributor level or a people leader, an entrepreneur, or someone not currently in the workforce.

Take a moment to think about your best manager/supervisor, someone you look up to. What did you admire about them? What qualities made you want to follow their lead? Now, think about whether you exhibit those behaviors and model them for your teams, family, and friends.

My favorite bosses demonstrated consistency in behavior (no surprises in how they reacted to good news or bad), took time to coach and mentor, taught by example, and were clear about their leadership philosophies and expectations.

I have internalized these qualities and have carried them across seven different companies. Each of the teams I had the privilege of leading, was different, each going through the uncertainty of a new leader coming into the organization and had perceptions based on their past experiences.

My first opportunity to model the behavior I wanted to see in others came within weeks of joining a newly acquired business as the department head of over 60 associates worldwide. One afternoon, two of my team members went in, and tentatively said: "We hate to bother you, but an issue has come up that you should know about."

I asked them to sit and started with, "It's okay, let's take it from the top, and I would appreciate your insights and any recommendations you have." They looked at each other, then described the issue. We had a good discussion and came away with a possible solution. Later each associate came to see me individually and said they had never expected that response from me, as prior leaders had either yelled at them or been accusatory. They were expecting fireworks and were hugely relieved at the reaction they got.

We may not know the perceptions or expectations people have of us based on their prior experiences, so manifesting the qualities of great leaders repeatedly and consistently defines how our teams perceive us, and how they will evolve.

Over time, my team saw consistency in my behavior and responses, they developed trust in me, and their style of managing issues took on a process-driven, resolution focused mindset.

From a practical perspective, I would offer the following:

1) Start from a position of trust. Your team/ associates/new acquaintances don't know you yet, but if you start from a position of trust, they will learn to trust you in return. My first business 1:1 with each person, begins with "You don't know me yet, please know that I trust you to do your best and come to me if I can help...I will work to earn your trust at your pace".

2) Define your top two or three guiding principles and make them your 'mantra.' For my last assignment, my top three were "Be Respectful, Be Process Driven, Be Accountable." These were purposefully defined, as the broader organization at the time was not as collaborative as they could be, and there existed pockets of the 'blame game.' By becoming process-driven within my department, I took blame out of the equation - not 'who made a mistake?' instead, 'what was the process supposed to be? Where was the gap? and how do we fix the process?'

3) Hold yourself and your team accountable to the defined principles and demonstrate every day that you are the best version of yourself.

The Un-Habit: Self-Doubt - also known as "your negative inner voice"

Why: Self-doubt, in the form of a negative inner voice, comes in many shapes and sizes and affects so many of us, and not just in our professional lives.

I was in a Starbucks line and noticed a well put together woman, perfect hair, beautiful outfit, and makeup. As I picked up my drink, I said, "You look amazing... have a lovely day". I started to walk away when she said, "Do you think so? I am just so nervous I have an interview and don't know if I will get the job". Wow. Not what I was expecting at all...her persona exuded self-confidence. I told her that and also said she needed to focus on what she DOES bring to the table, interview the company too...do they deserve her talent? It was wonderful to see her change her talk track right then. I do hope she got the perfect job for her.

Having given this example, I too had her doubts early in my career, my favorite being "you don't know enough"; there are of course many others; "you are not qualified for that job!", "What makes you think they will listen to you?" Pick your favorite.

As I went through my personal and professional jour-ney, external voices, well-meaning though they may have been, added to the self-doubt. During lunch one day, I bought myself some sunflowers. Coming back to the office, a co-worker asked, "Ooh! Who sent you those?" when I answered, "I bought them 'cos they are so happy!" I was offered, "I'm sorry, you will meet someone wonderful to buy you those one day." If I let it, my inner voice would have talked me into not enjoying those happy sunflowers. Instead, I smiled and recognized that comment for what it was - fear of being alone in the person, not a commentary on my state of mind.

I learned to recognize that voice and kept going despite all the negativity. As it turns out, I could change my talk track. For every negative thought, I have a positive one in its place. I am absolutely a 'glass half full' person, I believe wholeheartedly in choosing my own "Happy."

A couple of tips that helped me and may be of use to you:

- When the negative whispering voice turned up its volume, recognize it, acknowledge it, and said the word "Stop!" out loud.
- Take a moment to think about what you DO bring to the table, what you ARE good at, what you HAVE achieved.
- Acknowledge, yes, there are misses, and we make mistakes, but recognize that you came from a place of empowerment, not a place of fear in your decision-making.
- At any given time, you make the best decision you can, based on the information you have and

the research you have done. Then trust the best
to happen for you.

Once you recognize your negative inner voice for what it is, self – doubt, and silence it with the amazing power of YOU... you will change your world!

About Neelu: Neelu Gibson is the Co-Founder and President of SeaglassRQA, a boutique consulting house enabling companies to bring innovative medical devices to patients everywhere. During her 22+year tenure at Johnson & Johnson, Neelu led, coached and mentored over 100+ associates and was recognized through multiple awards for her leadership. Neelu is passionate about personal and professional development and continues to share her leadership experiences and learnings with individuals and groups

19

BUILD YOUR TRIBE ON STRENGTH, NOT SPITE - KELLY BYRNES

The Habit: Build your tribe on strength, not spite

By Kelly Byrnes - President and CEO of Voyage
Consulting Group

Why: There are three reasons this habit is important. First, strong women move mountains, figuratively, and build organizations, communities, and households literally. But, they don't do it alone.

Accomplishing great things always requires support. Whether it is support or reinforcement for idea-generating, financial backing, logistics, or cheerleading, everyone who accomplishes big things has had a tribe.

If you want to be an action-taker, build your tribe by joining women who are strong in their values and whose values align with yours. For example, join women who want to build a company or those who want to improve your neighborhood or those who want to grow your church community. When they want to take actions for the same reasons you do, and not for their self-serving reasons, they could become your tribe. Please pay close attention to the people you surround yourself with, as you will become like them. If they are strong-willed and focused on action, you will be too.

On the other hand, if your tribe is petty or competitive, it's likely to do more talking than achieving. People who spend time criticizing others, wallowing about the past, or speculating negatively about someone else, will not be action-oriented. They will be mediocre performers with reputations no one wants to align with for their future.

Sometimes, it seems like people expect women to be petty and competitive, rather than strong and supportive. Do not believe it!

Sure, some women are overly competitive, but there are plenty of women who want to move mountains and want to join forces. Seek them out and build relationships with them. Let the ones who bad-mouth other women (or men!) hang out with each other in their circle of mediocrity while you and the strong women make things happen.

The second reason this Habit matter relates to action. They (whoever "they" is) say, "If you want something done, give it to a busy person." When your tribe is based on strength, they will get things done. They will focus on relevant issues, devise a plan of attack, and make something happen. Stick with the strong ones because their tenacity will enable them to figure out how to move mountains.

The third reason this habit matters is because of resilience. If you are a woman of action, you can expect obstacles in your way. Build your resilience potential by anticipating adversity as best you can and rely on your strong tribe to help you move forward. Strong women don't get stuck in adversity. They recognize it, take lessons from it, and create a path forward. Be a woman like that and surround yourself with women like that.

When you build your tribe based on strength, you will be stronger.

The Un-Habit: Stop following the crowd

Why: I saw a t-shirt years ago that said, "If you're never the lead dog, your view never changes." Sometimes being the lead dog is tough. There's pressure choosing the direction, being on the front-line for obstacles that pop up and handling the needs of all the dogs. Lead dogs need to know what they are doing and where they are going.

As hard as leading is, being a follower all the time can suck the life out of a person.

I've seen many examples of follower burnout in the workplace. One person I worked with years ago was so afraid of leading and leadership that he just went along with everything without question. No matter the request or deadline, he just took it. While his attitude may have been applauded at first, by the time I met him, his reputation was nil. His lack of a backbone had caused poor quality control and several highly visible errors. By not speaking up, he let others take over his schedule, which caused conflicts and demoralized him. He left work every day resentful. Think how that attitude would affect his family and personal life. Yet, he returned the next day carrying his load of resentment back in to the workplace.

Sometimes, it is better to speak up and stop following along. Understand when that would be in your life. Base your decision to speak up on your core values.

Another example early in my career was when a vendor offered me a kick-back if he won the contract for the upcoming year. I was flabbergasted and awkwardly ended the meeting. I did not want to work with him, but management had other ideas. It occurred to me years later that they were probably getting a kick-back. Since it was my decision, we severed the relationship with the vendor, and my lesson was to stick with my core values and not just follow along.

That lesson came to mind years later when another ethical issue arose. This time it was related to inconsistent management practices. Like the earliest situation, I stuck with my core values and resisted the temptation to follow along. Again, some people were not thrilled; however, it worked out in the end.

. . .

IF YOU'RE NEVER the lead dog, you rely on others to determine your path. I encourage women of action not to do that. Don't go along without thinking.

Of course, it is wise to go along with the crowd sometimes. Just do so deliberately and not out of habit, fear, or lethargy.

About Kelly: Kelly Byrnes has loved business and leadership since she was a child. From pretending her Barbies were lawyers and architects of office buildings to her first "job" stocking shelves at the tiny store down the street at eight years old to double shifts at a department store during college, Kelly has loved business. For thirty years, she has had a distinguished career in operations, marketing, strategic planning, and Human Resources for large and mid-sized professional services and technical companies.

Today, Kelly is President and CEO of Voyage Consulting Group. Her unique business background enables Kelly to understand the needs of companies and executives in all functional areas. She brings her keen insights to Voyage's organization culture and executive development practices.

Kelly is an adjunct professor in the MBA program for Rockhurst University and serves as an executive coach for the University's Executive MBA program. She is a contributor to Forbes.com, the author of three books, and an award-winning national speaker.

Kelly's undergraduate work in history and business at Saint Mary's College, Notre Dame and her graduate work (MBA) at Rockhurst University laid the groundwork for her diverse career path and amplified her interest in leadership behaviors in business. She holds the SPHR and SHRM-SCP designations, and she graduated from The Players Workshop Improv program in Chicago.

Kelly currently serves on the board for Central Exchange, a nonprofit professional development organization focused on women, leadership, and diversity and inclusion. Kelly's volunteer work revolves around her church, women, education, and dogs.

On a personal note, Kelly is married to Bob, an Air Force veteran and retired fire captain. They live in Kansas City with their dog, Bebe. They enjoy spending time with their daughter in Montana, gathering with family in Kansas City and Pittsburgh, and cheering for Notre Dame football, Pittsburgh Penguins hockey, and Kansas City's Royals and Chiefs.

20

SAY YES EVERYDAY! - LAURA J. BRANDAO

The Habit: Say Yes Everyday!

By Laura J. Brandao - President of AFR, Inc.

Why: Have you ever wished that you could design your life? Well, I feel you can! It all starts with a mindset; each morning, as we awake, we have choices to make. Do we put our life on auto-pilot and repeat yesterday, or do we create a new habit where life becomes an adventure, and we begin to design our own life? Here's how it works: As you go through your day, think about what you can say YES to. We all have the ability to design our minutes/hours/days, etc. but we choose comfort just because it's more challenging to open yourself up to the unknown, and we haven't used our YES muscle enough. Even the smallest change to your routine can show you something that can alter your reality. Start small like speaking to a stranger and actually listening to them or asking someone a question where you were afraid to open up previously. As you see successes, your Yes's will get bigger and bolder. We are all creatures of habit, but this is not a positive feature, our minds and souls need to be challenged for us to create new memories and opportunities.

Frederic Buechner said, One life on this earth is all that we get, whether that is enough or not enough, and the obvious conclusion would seem to be that at the very least we are fools if we do not live it as fully and bravely and as beautifully as we can.

As you go about your day, think about what you are going to say yes to today, almost like a game, your life adventure. In July 2019, I started a blog; this allowed me to not only say yes every day but to take a moment at the end of the day to reflect on what I said yes to and watch the positive ripple that grew from all of the prior yes's. See, as humans, we go through life saying that we don't have enough, enough time, enough money, enough energy, that is actually the opposite of what we have, we have the ability to SAY YES to LIFE! A say yes everyday attitude is not saying yes because we expect to be rewarded, by saying yes every day we have to be open to saying yes to that moment in time that you will never get back with no expectations or preconceived notions. I challenge you to open up your mind and your heart to a say yes everyday attitude and keep a daily log of what you said yes to because your life will never be the same once you realize that you have the power to design your perfect life!

The Un-Habit: Not setting goals

Why: Why are we afraid to set goals? Yes, afraid, I said it we all know that we should and we even want to but it scares us because if we put it out to the world and we fail it's worse than not having a goal. But is that truly the case? NO! When we are children we have big dreams and unlimited possibilities. Our family tells us that we can and be anything we want but then life happens. Rejection and failure comes into our lives and we quickly lose our "can do" attitude for fear of failure and disappointment. Why should we set goals? We live in a glorious time, we have access to unlimited resources and communication platforms but we fall into routine and comfort zones that stop us from meeting our full potential. By setting daily, weekly, yearly and lifetime goals we can stay on a path that will build momentum and failure is only a lesson for us to learn to get us to the next phase of our goal. Our greatest fear should not be not achieving our goals it should be staying the same and wasting a day.

Setting goals is a great way of staying focused on our plans and creating momentum through actions. Some think that goals have to be life-changing epiphanies but even small accomplishments give us a sense of joy that shows us that we can do it. Don't overthink it and never be afraid of sharing your goals with the world because when you feel proud and powerful everyone you touch will benefit.

. . .

How to set goals and make them happen!

1- Close your eyes and think about what you would like to bring into your life.

2- Write down what came into your mind - Don't over-think it!

3- Share it! Telling someone will increase the likelihood that you will execute on it.

4 - Plan your 1st step, this is the most important. Getting started and accomplishing the 1st step will give you the confidence to keep going.

5- CELEBRATE! You don't have to get to the end to take a moment and reflect. Celebrate it with your tribe/community and if someone doesn't support your success you have just realized that they are not part of your tribe.

6- Keep GOING!

About Laura: Laura J. Brandao is the President and the only woman partner of AFR, (a national mortgage lender). Armed with a decade of experience, determination and belief in herself Laura J. Brandao started AFR Wholesale in 2007 during the mortgage meltdown and she had her high heel in the door and never turned back. Laura is one of the 2019 NJ top women in business award winner, she has been recognized in Housing Wires 2019 & 2018 Women of Influence, 2019 & 2018 Most Powerful women and a 2019 Women with Vision award winner and she is the chairwoman of the Women's Mortgage Network and an inaugural member of the Women empowering women organization. In April 2018 Laura underwent a transformation when she started to write a book. As she detailed out her story, she realized that most of her success both personally and professionally was due to a "say yes everyday" mindset. So, she started to test her theory, since that day Laura has become the President of AFR, she is a board member of a Silicon Valley technology company, she started her own podcast, Positively Charged Biz and has moderated 14 panel discussions, been an expert panelist 12 times and has been a pod cast guest 21 times and by the end of the first 12 months she was a key note speaker at the Bellagio in Vegas with an audience of 2000. The biggest thing that Laura has learned is that if you go into every situation with no preconceived notions or expectations you can do ANYTHING!

21

PRACTICE GRATITUDE DAILY - JENNIFER PRUETT

The Habit: Practice Gratitude Daily

By Jennifer Pruett - Creator of Mind Design

Why: In 2016, One year into my "entrepreneurial" journey, I had experienced a 6 figure financial loss and was in the midst of a very strained marriage. One day at an event, someone gave me the book "The Secret" by Rhonda Byrne. That night I started reading it, and I immediately took it to heart. It completely changed my perception of how I was looking at my results, and I went from focusing on failure to focusing on all that I had. I took the gratitude challenge, and after the first 28 days, my life and my business started to change. I began to see shifts in my thinking, which resulted in shifts in my business. It affected me so much that

I bought over 70 books and started giving them away to friends and other entrepreneurs. I took it further, and I began to share the book challenges via social media about four times a year. This year I created Greatness Through Gratitude, A Facebook Group for anyone who wants to share appreciation and gratitude as well as struggles or challenges they might be having. There isn't a morning that goes by that I don't start with gratitude and appreciation for all that I have. I feel as though I have been given a secret, and I must share it with the world.

As an entrepreneur, we have to be able to fail forward and not give up. Gratitude is the best way to become resourceful and push through the lessons.

When you cultivate gratitude, it will exponentially and positively affect every area in your life. Miracles have been reported in health as a result of choosing to focus on what IS working in your body and having an appreciation for that over-focusing on what's not working in your body. In creating a business, it's easy to get distracted and feel like it's not happening quick enough, however with gratitude as the focus, you change your perception to what is working on your business, and you are more creative in the creating. You come from a place of empowerment. In relationships, you can cultivate appreciation even with a challenging personality because there is always something to find to be grateful for.

After I found the book and started seeing its magic happen in my life, I began to see all the other 6 and 7 figure entrepreneurs that had the habit of cultivating gratitude and appreciation.

The Un-Habit: Procrastination

Why: "Procrastination" is derived from the Latin verb procrastinare — to put off until tomorrow. But it's more than just voluntarily putting things off until later.

Procrastination equals death in business.

We procrastinate when we feel fear, anxiety, or doubt about a task that needs to get accomplished. We become overwhelmed by the challenge of the task, and instead of breaking it down to smaller chunks, we get stuck, create excuses, and we don't ask ourselves the right empowering questions to generate our desired result. You can overcome fear, doubt, and procrastination through consistent action. As an entrepreneur, it's extremely vital that you stay in action both in and on your business. Action creates clarity. Sometimes we get so busy working in our business doing things that are not money-making activities (because they are fun like accepting lunch invitations) that we avoid doing the things that are vital to generating income like making sales call, creating a P&L, balancing the books or making videos. The task seems daunting and difficult, and we get stuck in procrastination. We then allow our thoughts of fear, and doubt dictate our directions. Six months later, your business is either stuck or losing income. However, when you stay in action, every single day, just doing three things that will move your business forward, you will thrive. You will move through the fear and doubt, and you will grow your business much more quickly than if you stay in procrastination. Once you understand how to stay in action, you create clarity, and you will learn how to ask yourself empowering questions like "whom do I know that can help me with this." You become much more resourceful, and you are clear to create.

Each morning ask yourself, what three things can I do today to move my business ahead?

About Jennifer: Jennifer Pruett started her career as a retail store manager, managing multi-million dollar stores all over the west coast. At the birth of her first in 2014 daughter Cayden, she realized how valuable her time was and wanted to learn how to trade her money for her time so she could be with her family more.

She started as a real estate investor. In her first year, she had a devastating 6 Figure loss, and she quickly discovered how to fail forward. Refusing to get a job, she went on to do over 100 real estate transactions. She joined a local REI community with an earn while you learn program and started generating $10K, $20K months, helping others avoid the mistakes she had made. After attending a local networking group where they were reading T Harv Eker, one of her mentors at the time gave her "The Science Of Getting Rich," and her love of helping others on their mindset began. She loves the real estate, but she learned on her journey that results in your business are the product of your thoughts. She created Mind Design to help other entrepreneurs master their inner game so they can have a business and a life of ultimate success.

UPDATE AND REVIEW MY CALENDAR - JESSICA DEMUMBRUM

The Habit: Update and review my calendar

By Jessica DeMumbrum - Financial Agent

Why: I continuously refer to my calendar and review it each night before bed. I wake up and get out of bed quicker, knowing my goals for the day. When I review my calendar, it keeps my mind moving, and I look for ways to save time and group activities together and get more out of each day. Looking at: activities, phone calls, and people's names keeps new ideas forming in my head. A simple idea appears, and I jot it down, then another and another. As my different ideas begin to compound, I either wind up with several directions to move in, or the ideas suddenly brainstorm into one; I see something I had not before. All of the single ideas will wake me up at night, with my head trying to sort them out. I need to write the impulse thoughts down before I fall back asleep and do not remember "the greatest idea EVER." Once I wake up in the morning, I like to set a pair of "fresh eyes" on the calendar and review it. This again gets me ready to start my day, and I look forward to making each thing happen. I get a great sense of accomplishment when I put a check-mark next to all activities as I complete them. I draw a line through and write "canx" next to anything canceled. I circle anything that will have to be done later and imme-diately reschedule it on the calendar. I do not draw a line through any circle until it is done. The calendar I keep is a leather-bound paper calendar with tons of space for daily note-taking. I need all of this space for drawings as well as notes and math problems.

Since I am visual: doodle art, ticks in a row, or something abstract, has solved some mighty complicated circum-stances. Being able to look at an entire week and a whole month, all at once, really clicks with my way of thinking. Seeing my writing triggers old thoughts, where typing does not. Even a messy, disorganized page of notes and drawings on a page brings back exact details. Being able also to hold, touch, and flip through the pages, brings inspiration to my thinking. Keeping up with my calendar keeps me closer to what I do when it is with me, and I can flip it open in an instant.

I love my calendar. I would not say I obsess over it, but the more I study it, the more creative my mind becomes, and my efficiency increases.

The Un-Habit: Old Habits Die Hard

Why: The importance of defeating procrastination is due to its complete lack of rationality. Worry is imagination. I had a fear of failure or being lesser than my friends because they would treat me bad. I had learned to avoid things rather than to fail. Procrastination was the reason I would complete tasks at the absolute last second. Dread is why I would say, "I can do it tomorrow." and tomorrow would turn into two weeks. Procrastination is why I would not feel at ease because of this invisible monster looming over my head, disrupting my peace. I had all good intentions when saying, " I WILL GET THIS DONE TOMORROW!". Tomorrow turned into another day of avoiding what I dreaded — complete irrational thinking. Once the task at hand had to be done, I would sit down and begin to work. "Voila!"

"Done.", "That was easy." Then I would be ticked off and annoyed with myself for putting such a simple thing off. You would think I would learn. Nope. Old habits die hard. This habit is important to break because it is complete nonsense. An excellent way to break this habit (for me), ditch your old friends. The second is to realize; it is nothing to stress about. Approach the task right away. Complete tasks early to get them off your list. If it is a difficult task, definitely get started early and give yourself time to solve difficulties that could arise. When I broke this nasty habit, I had to stay focused, or it would sneak up on me again — my greatest way to avoid avoiding, yep, my calendar. I plan the start date, so I don't have too much going on. I highlight the halfway point encase I have fallen behind. I plan my completion date a week in advance of the due date. When I have the process planned out in advance, the guide keeps me on schedule, and I avoid: crunch time, feeling of doom, and less than my best quality work.

About Jessica: Jessica DeMumbrum comes from a military family and grew up in a small town located in the far, rural, east side of San Diego County. Working her way through community college, she worked minimum wage jobs that taught her how to work with the public and earn promotions. Three years as a corrections officer developed priceless people skills. Jessica volunteered for five years for the Sheriffs Department VIDA Program. VIDA serves as a paramilitary program for at-risk youth, 12-17 years old. She taught: self-discipline, drill, physical exercise and goal oriented classes on: self worth, team work, hard work and success in life. She served 12 years in the United States Marine Corps, three of which included tours during Iraqi Freedom and Enduring Freedom. The military increased her leadership skills with greater responsibility and personnel leadership skills. Next followed seven years as a franchise owner. Here, all people skills and problem solving skills proved valuable. Currently Jessica works as an independent agent for World Financial Group. As an agent she is challenged with the desire to help people plan for security and retirement. Jessica lives in the Mojave Desert and enjoys gardening and exercise.

23

GOING OUTSIDE DURING THE DAY INCREASES PRODUCTIVITY - LORI A. MCNEIL

The Habit: Going Outside During the Day Increases Productivity

By Lori A. McNeil - International Educator & Business Coach

Why: Imagine a work-life that has you under the confines of four solid walls and fluorescent lighting (watch the opening scene to the Tom Hanks movie "Joe Vs. The Volcano" for perspective). The oppression that occurs in that environment has been proven to reduce productivity, create a hostile work environment, and those conditions will eventually find their way to the doorsteps of your life, inviting themselves in. As entrepreneurs, there is even more of a draw to focus so much on what we need to do or to spend our days creating content that when we finally look up from our screens, we wonder where the day went.

How do you feel after a day spent at one of your favorite places, such as the beach, or perhaps on a mountaintop? Perchance you are a bicyclist or a runner, or maybe you love sitting at the park in the soft green grass watching your kids play. Wherever your happy place, each of us has at least one place...outdoors... that we can immediately think of heading to in order to 'escape' the doldrums of the norm. One habit that I implement daily to trick my mind into maintaining a consistent freedom mentality is to take regular breaks throughout my day and go outside. The fresh air, the warm sun (even through those winter days at times), a cool or warm breeze... these are the elements that protect me from creating a momentum of monotony that we all can easily fall into.

Getting outside forces our brain to take a break... an adult time out. The change of scenery allows our minds to clear out. The outside world shifts our brain, if only for the moment, long enough for us to refocus, find a fresh perspective, and to stimulate movement. As someone who loves what I do, and who was a teacher for many years I know what looking at four walls all day long can do to someone's thoughts, actions, perspectives, and life. Just a simple break, done a few times a day (even 5 minutes), will stimulate your creative mind. Outside breaks have allowed me at times to double my productivity in half the time. Put yourself in an event setting. Most of us have sat in professional events before...the ones that seem to go on forever without a break...How do you feel? You start to ask yourself when can I go to the bathroom, get something to drink, or whatever... yet you don't want to leave because you don't want to miss anything. Your brain does the same thing to you when you don't give it that break. Give it that break. Boost your productivity. You will see a difference. Your productivity will see a difference. Your business will see a difference. Your life will see a difference.

The Un-Habit: Believing Busy is Beneficial

Why: Stop. Just stop for a moment. Take 10 seconds and do nothing. Think about nothing. Did you do it? Chances are, you thought about something that 'needs' to be done. We have done ourselves a disservice to believe that if we keep ourselves busy, we can accomplish more. We tell others we are 'too busy' to take on something only to say yes to something else a few minutes down the road. Keeping ourselves in constant motion leads to weariness. Busyness takes away from our ability to perform well in the long run. The world is a marathon, yet we live like we are in a sprint to the finish line, only to find out when we get to the finish line, we have yet another lap to complete.

Busyness creates false outcomes. Busyness reduces productivity. The more we do... the more we do. And when we do more, there is less time to recover, to rest, to replenish, to renew, to rejoice in what we have accomplished. Productivity is beneficial; however, busyness does not consistently deliver benefits. More often than not, it delivers disaster. We end up having to redo work. Telling others that we are busy too often means that we have lost control of our routine, our schedule.... our minds. Busyness breeds burnout. Burnout leaves us empty, and disdain can set in. Pretty soon, what was once the passion that burned in us becomes the very thing that we detest. Sure there are deadlines to meet, presentations to prepare for, books to write, clients to care for, customers to satisfy... however, if we are not in top-notched condition, none of those effects will produce the benefit we started out to deliver.

About Lori: International Educator, Speaker, and Business Coach, Lori focuses on the missing foundational tools organizations need for long-term success. Experienced in public and private sectors, Lori helps new businesses grow and established companies re-strategize. She has successfully grown grassroots programs from zero to millions which lead to National recognition by U.S. Senator, Gordon Smith. Lori is also a Curriculum Designer, a retired Business Professor, and has helped grow countless organizations organically (including her own International company that includes Legacy Leaders Unlimited, Media Secrets, and Driven Mastery -- all brands that assist Entrepreneurs to build a true, long - lasting purpose). Lori has been featured on

ABC, NBC, CBS, FOX, & 500 various media outlets per year. She has authored several Best -Selling books; including co-authoring a Best-Selling book with Kevin Harrington, the original Shark of the hit TV show, Shark Tank and Pioneer of "As seen on TV." Lori works with organizations globally to support literacy, cancer research, young entrepreneurship, and military support programs. She was an invited guest at the National Celebration of Reading in Washington D.C where she helped raise over Three (3) Million Dollars for Literacy and was recently awarded the Lifetime Presidential Service Award for her long-term success in working with communities Nationally. Most recently, Lori was selected as one of the official featured speakers for the Think & Grow Rich World Tour and was honored with the prestigious Outstanding Business Coach Professional Award.

24

CHECK YOUR BLIND SPOTS DAILY (AWARENESS) - ELLA GLASGOW

The Habit: Check your blind spots daily (Awareness)

By Ella Glasgow- The Dream Ignitor

Why: We've all heard about the power of journaling. Sheesh, there's a journal for everything under the sun. But how often have you looked at your journal as a powerful tool for insight? Insight into you. Insight into your business.

I think every woman on the planet has kept a diary at some point in her life. I had one when I was a little girl. It was yellow with a fairy princess swinging on a tree. She had long flowing hair. And it had a little golden lock that could only be opened by a tiny golden key. But as I got older, I wrote less consistently in my diary. She was an old friend I'd grown farther away from.

That was until I rediscovered journaling.

At first, I wrote feverishly every day because I'd read somewhere that journaling was good to do. But I never stuck with it for longer than a month. Then, last year, I realized something about journaling that I hadn't thought of before, and maybe you haven't either.

Myself, currently, I keep a few different journals. One for brain dumping in the morning. One to outline the things I want out of life. One to keep track of things I'm grateful for. And one to keep track of things I've accomplished. The last one might be my favorite. I call it my "Ya Did List" It's to keep track of all the things ya did.

Ok, but what's this new insight I've found? In the space I dwell in, there's much talk about manifestation. That word in itself can be a trigger for many people. It sounds so woo woo voodoo.

Now, I love myself some woo woo, but I'm also about practicality. The word manifestation means that something is revealed in the natural world. That's my definition because good ol' Merriam & Webster were to abstract for my liking.

When something is manifested (or revealed), it doesn't necessarily mean it wasn't there before. It just means the person to whom it was revealed can now see it.

Ok, think I may have lost you on that one, so let me give ya another way to look at it. You remember the game Punch Buggy. I promise I won't tell anyone your age if you do (or if you don't). Punch buggy was that game we played on long car trips, and it was an excuse to punch your sister. No seriously, the game was to see who could find the most punch buggies (Volkswagon beetles) on the road. So you'd call out "punch buggy red" when you saw one and punch the person in the arm that was next to you.

Did you ever recognize that, before you started playing the game, you didn't necessarily see those particular cars on the road? But as soon as you guys were ready to play, suddenly, there were a plethora of punch buggies. They MANIFESTED. They were already there, but your awareness wasn't paying attention to them. You hadn't given it the command to look for punch buggies and so it "blocked" you from seeing them constantly.

So besides you now wanting to play punch buggy with a friend, what's any of that got to do with journaling?

EVERYTHING!

I realized that my journaling was a way for me to tap into my awareness on a level that was deeper than just thinking about it. I'm explicitly journaling now in a way that keeps me aware. I journal about the things I want to see more of in my life. I do call that journal My Manifestation Journal. Clever, I know.

Sometimes I write the same thing every day. Sometimes I write something brand new. But all the time I'm writing to my awareness. It's a game of punch buggy for myself (minus the arm punching because that would be weird).

This writing is not a set it and forget it. This is a way for me to check my blind spots. I often go back and review what I've written. I check to see how things are coming along. Do I need to be more clear? Can I make it more concise? I'm constantly revising. All of this is keeping my awareness of what I'm going after.

And eventually it just "shows up" But now you and I both know, it didn't just show up because we've got a journal that kept track of the whole journey.

The Un-Habit: Stop Undervaluing Yourself

Why: I challenge you to take the next five days to be acutely aware of your self-talk. It may seem to you that you are great with yourself, and you think and act positively.

But I would disagree.

If you've ever wondered why people aren't listening to you or why things don't seem to go your way, maybe this is where you should begin. At the end of the day, if you can't get behind your ideas, why should anyone else back you up.

So this week, as you're acutely aware, you're going to write down any talk you have in yourself, or outwardly that is not empowering. What does that mean? Any time you play that old record

"I'm not good at this" or

"I'm so stupid" or

"Why would I ever do something so dumb?"

You know the players. You sing every word of their songs over and over, and it's time for you to update your playlist.

You're going to record every time you hear that old record play. So keep a notebook handy. Or even better, make a note on your phone just for this purpose for the next five days.

Make sure you head each day with the date, so you know when that happened. At the end of 5 days, you're going to take account of every negative thing you've said to yourself. Every time you've shot your self down.

One of my clients realized when he first came to me that he was doing this to himself at work. He thought that he wasn't being listened to, and nobody wanted to hear him. And so, he was very frustrated.

We dug into his thought process and found out very quickly that he was his own enemy. Just that week, his boss had commented on an idea he had and said it was good and...

He shot his self down, telling his boss, "maybe we should go get some of the other guys to see what they think."

Do you hear that?

His boss JUST told him they should implement his idea, and HE shot

his

own

self

down.

We found out that it wasn't others who didn't value his ideas...it was HIM.

About Ella: Ella Glasgow is a professional vocalist, speaker, and a biz and life coach for undercover creatives. She's also the wife to a pastry chef and mommy to a precocious 4-year-old. Known as The Dream Ignitor, she's on a mission to pull up on the greatness in people to help them not only uncover their dreams but help them finally know how to make it possible to begin.

When her son was born in 2015, she realized that she had been holding back on her own dreams. As she looked into those precious eyes, she knew she didn't want to one day say to him "baby, you can do and be whatever you want to, but mommy can't" From that point forward she has been working toward her dreams and working with and encouraging others to do the same.

25

FOCUS ON 15 -GET MOVING FOR AT LEAST 15 MINUTES EACH DAY - CATHERINE TURLEY

The Habit: Focus on 15 - Get moving for at least 15 minutes each day.

By Catherine Turley - CEO of Fit Armadillo®, Bestselling Author, Podcast Host

Why: Want to change your world? The world? If you're a woman action-taker, I guess that the answer to this question is yes. But how do you do it? What consistent actions should you take and make part of your habit and day? My tip for you is to focus on 15-get moving for 15 minutes each day to find yourself moving closer to your big dreams.

I might be the CEO of a fitness company now, but I used to hate fitness because fitness meant gym class. I was so uncoordinated that as a kindergartener, I would have tried to run away from home if you told me I'd spend most of my 20s working in gyms.

Then? I found running in middle school. I didn't need to be coordinated to do it, and thanks to some significant running genes from my dad, I was a decent runner. Fitness became fun for me when I found this activity that I enjoyed doing.

Fast forward a few years, and I went to college. Do you believe that I was still afraid of the gym then? Well, I was EVEN when my roommate was trying to get me to take a group fitness class. I had no interested because I had running and was terrified of the gym.

One bad breakup and a few too many chocolate covered gummy bears later, I finally gave in to her request and agreed to try ONE class. It felt great! I was so surprised and excited, I got a class pass and became a regular participant. In my senior year, I became a certified fitness instructor and personal trainer, so I could help my friends enjoy what I had found. I'd had a similar experience with wanting to share running with my friends, but not everyone took to it, so I was eager to share more.

Over the years, I've had the honor to share different fitness options and knowledge with hundreds of clients and class participants, and I've seen, again and again, the huge positive change in their moods when they finish a workout.

How does this relate to you?

Well, when I took my action taking into starting my own fitness company, Fit Armadillo, I started befriending other women action takers, other female entrepreneurs. Over and over again, I heard stories of how they had let their health go and given up their fitness routine for the sake of building their empire. The business was booming, but they felt horrible. They didn't want to take business photos; they lacked energy. My heart broke for them, and I started the Fitting in Fitness interview series with women who weren't in the fitness industry but had used movement as a secret weapon of sorts to enjoy more creativity, energy, and productivity in their businesses.

My journey speaking with these women and later the superwomen who shared similar stories in my book, *Superwomen Secrets Revealed*, has proven to me the power that moving has when it comes to wanting to move towards your big dreams and change your world and then the world.

Richard Branson has even shared that he finds his fitness routine (which often isn't very routine!), is what helps him be more productive.

Anecdotal evidence aside, science backs up these stories!

When we use our muscles, more of our nerve cells fire, and we liberate more of the neurotransmitters norepinephrine, serotonin, and dopamine. What neurotransmitters do we target with stimulants when we have attention problems? Norepinephrine and dopamine! This is NOT a coincidence!

So the next time you feel overwhelmed, tired, stressed out, uncreative, lacking focus, or just down, think of this: focus on 15! Get moving for 15 minutes and get excited. You might just come back with your next BIG idea that will change the world.

For help along the journey, you can tune into my podcast, The Fit Fifteen. I'm SO passionate about this habit that yes, I created a podcast show designed to help you get moving for 15 minutes.

I hope you enjoy it, and I can't wait to hear how this habit changes your world for the better.

The Un-Habit: Overbooking yourself

Why: In this nonstop 24/7 world, it's easy to overbook yourself, so you don't miss out on an opportunity, especially if you're a self-proclaimed woman action-taker. I get it! I've had and have been affected by FOMO (fear of missing out) when it comes to activities in my personal and professional life and has often wondered if I know how to say "no." When I've finally taken the time to pause, look at my goals, and ask myself what events and activities make sense and are aligned with my longterm plan, I not only make better choices, but I'm able to be more present in the events I'm a part of. This makes me happier, and as my favorite positive psychologist and bestselling author Shawn Achor has shared, happiness is what leads to success. When you're happy and not frantic, you feel better, and people and opportunities are drawn to you. When you aren't overbooked, you're able to take the time to fit in fitness, which also helps lead to more happiness. Remember, you don't need to get moving for an hour every day or go to the gym. Focus on 15 - 15 minutes at least once a day for more happiness, energy, and focus as you take action in all areas of your life.

About Catherine: Catherine Turley, M.Ed is the CEO of Fit Armadillo®, Bestselling author of *Superwomen Secrets Revealed: Successful Women Talk About Fitting in Fitness and Dare You to Join Them*, and host of the featured podcast, The Fit Fifteen. Although she's been an ACE-Certified personal trainer for over a decade, she grew up dreaming of ways to get out of gym class. Her years of toiling in the gym have made her a passionate ally of those who want to get in shape but feel uncomfortable in the gym environment. Ultimately, it led to the creation of her company, Fit Armadillo®, whose mission is to help busy individuals find fitness they can enjoy at their own place and pace. Armed with her B.S. Degree in Biology from The College of William and Mary, Catherine enjoys debunking fitness and nutrition myths to help her clients achieve lasting results and uncover the many benefits of an active lifestyle. Catherine has been quoted for her expertise in WebMD magazine, on Spark-People.com, LiveStrong.com, EmpowHER, Fitbie, and WorldLifestyle, and writes as a blogger for the Huffington

Post and Thrive Global. Catherine has zero tolerance for diets, supplements, and detoxes (and not just because she's a huge fan of gluten-full bread!), but lots of love for those new to fitness. An avid runner and Boston Marathon qualifier, she has competed in races from the 1500m to the full marathon, and loves helping others start a running routine. While no longer a classroom teacher, Catherine enjoys using her Master's in Education from The University of Connecticut to promote literacy as a volunteer tutor in local schools. She's also passionate about sharing fitness with the next generation and enjoys coaching and fundraising for the nonprofit, Girls on the Run.

26

COMPARTMENTALIZING YOUR WAY TO SANITY - BREAKING DOWN YOUR EVERYDAY ROLES INTO BITE-SIZE PIECES IN ORDER TO LIVE A MORE HARMONIOUS LIFE - DIANA BARBIANI

The Habit: Compartmentalizing your way to Sanity - breaking down your everyday roles into bite-size pieces in order to live a more harmonious life

By Diana Barbiani - Small Business Consultant and Sales Professional

Why: Daily (most days), I find myself overwhelmed with life's responsibilities. I am currently juggling full time highly demanding sales job, a side hustle, two young kids, commitment to fitness and healthy diet, time with friends as well as my newly found romantic life. I consider these to be the five pillars of my life. And if you are anything like me, you want to be acing all of them, at all times! Excellent idea, but let's admit, the adulting can be such a drag sometimes. Like, let me stay in bed today, please.

It was during an especially busy time, such as the holiday season that's upon us, that I inadvertently and probably as a part of the much-needed self-care system started a great little habit. Naturally, it was unnamed at first. But then, hidden deep in my memory from all that couples-therapy session I went through, did I find a perfect term for my little habit. COMPARTMENTALIZING. Dictionary explains it as "Dividing into sections". For me, it translates to "Staying Sane."

Here is how it works; anytime I start feeling like my anxiety is getting the best of me, I pause and check-in. Usually, I start with the good news first, and that is pretty much always my health. I say a quick gratitude prayer for being healthy, strong, able. If I had a headache that week, I acknowledge it and move on. If my knee bothered me because I went for a long run, I remember that the pain was temporary.

Next, it's my kiddos; they are happy, healthy, growing up too fast. I recall the weekend and all the fun we had shopping for craft supplies, coming home, and making art. Then we watched a movie, ate pizza and popcorn. Good times.

My mind races, and naturally goes to my work next, but I pushed it away, for now. The reason being that my work is most likely the main reason why I needed to develop this type of habit in the first place. Always working, earning, climbing. Work is a big deal around here.

The thought that comes on next is whether I have been spending enough quality time with my friends lately.

With my family still living back in Europe, friends I choose here are my family. I much cherish our moments together. I recall my commitment to a lovely chill evening over a glass of wine, or two, with the few of my besties. I love it when we stay in, talk, and share. It's best, and the cheapest form of therapy money can buy.

And then I start thinking of my man, the new bright spot in my life. We have some much in common but keep uncovering something new about each other every day. I think I'm in love again.

So, finally, my mind takes me to that dreadful, dark place, of thinking I'm not enough, maybe because I've got another "NO" from the buyer or missed sales goal that was unattainable, to begin with. My mind spirals out of control, and for a second, all the good thoughts I previously had are gone with the wind. I start doubting all my success, prescribing it to luck, stable economy, good weather, or whatever crazy thing I concocted in my mind, instead of admitting that is all part of hard (and smart) work, grit and hunger that's poured into everything I do. As I start feeling the storm subsiding, my "first world problems" getting smaller by the second, my heart rate slows down to normal. I am alive, happy, healthy, present. Life is good.

The Un-Habit: Paralysis of Analysts - how over-thinking and under-doing are hindering your true potential

Why: We all know the type; the dreamers, the infinite

idea-pitchers, the wannabe entrepreneurs. There is excitement in their voice, they show high enthusiasm for their work, and their charisma is contagious to those around them. They give a great speech on how and why their project, product, or business venture will bring big dollars, gain popularity, or change the world. They may have a valid point or even a life-changing idea, but that's all they stay, ideas. They are all talk, backed with zero action. The case is, those individuals most likely stumbled upon something great, but never took a leap of fate, and just went for it. They got stuck on the 1st step, and never moved on. Is it fear of failure? Lack of commitment, time, or money? Whatever prevents them from moving forward is exactly what keeps them stuck on that hamster wheel. They are the drivers of their own (mis)fortune.

So, what is a girl to do about this nasty little habit that inhibits us all, either in the form of procrastination or as merely getting stuck on that 1st step? I humbly suggest creating milestones and attaching the deadline on each. Yes, marking the actual date for each step needed to be executed, or making it public; either announcing it to a few of your best friends or posting it on your social media. Even the best of us need someone to keep us accountable. Of course, one of the surest ways you will get your idea off the ground this time is to find yourself a mentor. They have the experience, are willing to share the knowledge and guide you through the process. They've done it all before and are most likely honored to be a part of your journey.

Therefore, START. If you are fully committed to

achieving the success that you deserve, the whole universe conspires to help you along the way.

 **About Diana:** I am originally from Croatia, a quaint little gem nestled along the Adriatic Sea. Not quite famous (or expensive) as Italy or Greece, but none the less breathtaking. Croatia is home to over 1000 islands, many world heritage and historic sites. My life brought me to the US back in 1998, and I landed right here in beautiful sunny San Diego. I found my first job shortly after finishing my English language courses. It was a retail job in a local art gallery that thought me many things about fine art, artist, and patrons. It was a wonderful introduction in sales, which will end up being my career till this day.

Since 2001, I've worked as an inside sales rep for a local apparel company. Over the years, I was fortunate enough to get involved in product design as we import our own goods, as well as retail design, where I get the opportunity to plan, design and oversee the opening of our retail locations. Along with our purchasing department, I visit trade shows, to source out the best and brightest apparel and souvenirs, to be sold in our stores. We currently run and operate 12 retail stores located in Gaslamp, Belmont Park, Old Town, Coronado, and Oceanside.

My latest venture is helping small business owners succeed in ever-changing market. I teach workshops and

conduct 1-on-1 client advising for the two local procure-
ment agencies. I get to meet some amazing people, who
work hard to contribute the local economy. I am proud
and honored to be a part of that initiative. My expertise is
gaining retail distribution, specifically in the military
market. Through my work, I hope to share years of experience with a fellow business owner, and keep the businesses open.

27

BE BOLD, BE DIFFERENT, BE YOU! - KATIE MARES

The Habit: Be Bold, Be Different, Be YOU!

By Katie Mares - Co-Founder, Chief Inspirational Officer
Alkamey Group

Why: It was a cold November afternoon. I had just walked out of a Toast Masters Meeting and had started my car when the phone rang. It was a mentor of mine. I remember being excited to pick up that particular call and have an energizing conversation. Unfortunately, that wasn't what was in store for me. In a serious tone, he said: "Katie, I wanted to talk to you about your chances of making it in a male-dominated industry (the speaking and consulting industry)." Of course, I was open to hearing any feedback so I said: "ok, go for it." He continued to say "well you don't speak up enough when in group settings and you're too young and pretty to be taken seriously."

If you were peering through the window of my car you would've seen my jaw drop. I was shocked and couldn't believe what I was hearing. The rest of the conversation followed the same tone. I ended the conversation by saying "I am proud of who I am, what I represent, and if my looks (or being a young woman) is going to affect my chances of getting a client; then maybe they are not the right client for me." I hung up the phone feeling infuriated, but also insanely motivated. That conversation kicked my ass into high gear and I never looked back. I seized that defining conversation and used it as fuel to be the best version of myself by vowing to be bold, to be different, all while remaining true to myself.

Daring to be bold, different, and unapologetically yourself will only propel you forward. Instilling this habit and positive self-narrative will unleash the awesomeness that is you. Every time you try to fit into the mould others think you should fit into, you are chipping away at your authenticity which greatly affects how you show up in your life. You were put on this earth as a beautiful woman and you should embrace every bit of your femininity. By embracing the simple fact that EVERYONE is different and those differences are what make this world a beautiful (and interesting) place will only elevate your potential. Take bold steps, own your unique qualities, and always show up as yourself; because you are perfect just the way you are.

I don't share this advice without having fought my way through the sea of men that have crashed against me like waves in the roughest ocean. I give you this counsel because every time I tried to fit the mould of what was expected, I failed. I have had numerous 'square peg, round hole moments in my personal and professional life. My success came to me when I decided to show up in a bold way, honoring my differences, and never wavering from being me.

Today I have broken through the mostly male-dominated automotive industry. I am a speaker, trainer, and consultant; and I was NEVER, not even for one second, anyone else but myself.

In those very cold moments in my car, I swore that I would not let anyone and their perceptions of me hold me down, and neither should you.

I urge you to BE BOLD, BE DIFFERENT, BE YOU

The Un-Habit: Stop thinking with a scarcity mentality

Why: The mean girls club exists. I have experienced firsthand. It wasn't too long ago that I was told that the 'ladies' don't want me to succeed, and I have been 'blacklisted' from a few speaking events because I wasn't part of the in-crowd. These ladies were virtually holding my speaking career hostage because I was the new girl on the block. I, of course, thanked my friend for her honesty. However, I was bewildered by this conversation. It's bad enough that women have to fight an uphill battle on our raise to equality, but to have to also worry about a battle within our own gender is a disgrace. How are we to win the war on equality if women don't support, guide, and refer to each other?

This world is full of opportunities. Unfortunately for women, there are fewer of these opportunities to obtain, or are there? Being a female entrepreneur has widened my eyes to the lack of opportunity we create for ourselves and others because we approach opportunities from a place of scarcity. I have found that when an opportunity presents itself, we hold it so close as if someone is going to steal it right from under our nose. Worse than that is there is a lack of support, encouragement, and referrals between women because of the fear that holds us hostage. This fear cultivates a scarcity mindset, which in turn hinders our progress rather than catapulting us forward. The day I found out that I had been 'blacklisted' lit a flame inside me. I now have a burning passion for stopping the scarcity mindset among women (and humans in general) by being radically honest and having the tough conversations most are afraid to have. But more importantly, I will show up with an abundance mindset helping those that cross my path.

Acting with a scarcity mentality only limits the abundance that the world has to offer not only for yourself but for the women that surround you. As women, our actions support a scarcity mindset, and we often do this without knowing it; we do this because we are afraid to miss an opportunity for ourselves. We have been conditioned this way. There are Only 21% of executives are female after all.

Imagine a world, however, where we lifted each other, passed opportunities to others, and celebrated success in others. The world would be full of light, new chances to succeed, and more women at the top. Abundance provides a positive ripple effect where a scarcity mindset stops you dead in your tracks. Which world would you rather contribute to?

If you could break one habit, stop thinking with a scarcity mentality. By thinking bigger than yourself, you will not only help others succeed, but you will also intensify your future opportunities

 **About Katie:** Katie knows first hand the challenges organizations and their encounter as they strive to design a customer service program that is sustainable and has an impact in the marketplace. She also knows that developing a program is just one small step to success, it is the tools and implementation plan that makes a program take flight.

Using her experiences as a Chief Inspiration Officer, building company infrastructure and designing customer experience programs, Katie is now a leading voice inspiring positive, actionable change in the organizations she partners with. Katie has earned her Master's in Adult

Training and Development and is a Certified Training & Development Professional.

Katie lives in Toronto with her family. When she is not traveling around the world consulting and speaking, Katie can be found on a yoga mat (in a shoe store!) or snuggled on the couch with her three little ones eating homemade popcorn and watching a movie!

28

GET A LITTLE UNCOMFORTABLE - CHELLIE W. PHILLIPS

The Habit: Get a little uncomfortable

By Chellie W. Phillips - Author, Speaker and Successfully Ever After Career Coach

Why: I am what I am today because of what I believed about myself yesterday, and I'll be tomorrow what I believe about myself right now.

I've searched and can't find who to attribute that quote to, but it's one I wrote out on an index card and kept where I see it often.

It struck me how much truth is in that statement. How we start each day, week, month, or year is important. Our vision of ourselves and our abilities do shape the path ahead.

You've got to be willing to put the strength of your belief to the test. Just like you go to the gym to build up your muscles, you can do the same thing with the belief in yourself. When you trust your vision and make an effort to bring it to life, it seems things and people show up to help you along the way.

HOW BIG IS YOUR DREAM?

I fear most people don't believe big enough. You need that big dream to stretch and grow you. You need failures to learn from. You need to hurt to learn how not to treat people along the way.

When you wake up in the morning, I'd like to challenge you to believe in that big dream. If you're like me, it's hard to believe for more when you're comfortable. I'm here to tell you, get uncomfortable. Be a little afraid of what you want to achieve. There's fear in the unknown. That fear is what keeps us stationary. If you believe you'll achieve something, you begin adding things into your day that moves you closer and closer to that goal. You seek out people who encourage you or help guide you. You learn new skills. You find extra minutes in the day to do a little more that moves you toward your destination.

The opposite is also true. If you tell yourself you can't, you won't. If you look for all the obstacles, that's all you'll see. Your vision is either one of opportunity or roadblocks.

. . .

Roadblocks aren't stop signs.

I'm not saying the road will always be a smooth one. Sure there will be obstacles along the way. It's how you approach them that makes all the difference. You either back up, make a left turn, and try to find a new path, or you can choose to sit there and watch someone else achieve your dream. Don't let one failure stop your progress. Yes, it sucks when something doesn't go right. It hurts when you learn people don't always have your back. The key is not to allow that to become your focus. It takes your eyes off where you want to go. Use those as lessons of how not to approach something or how to better pick your support force. It's only a hard stop if you choose to quit moving forward.

Upgrade your mindset

It's time to upgrade your mindset. I believe there's a real power in this process. Seeing it and actively seeking it makes your brain look for ways to make it possible. Your belief is the fuel. You'll start acting differently. You'll begin making choices based on your belief.

Ask yourself what would bring you genuine happiness. Ask yourself what you want to obtain. How do you see yourself growing? What is it you'd love to be doing? You can make it happen. Pick your first step. Focus on it. Once you've made that one, keep moving forward. Don't get hung up trying to get there all at once. Slow and steady will get you there.

So I'll ask you...what will you believe this year?

The Un-Habit: Quit waiting for Monday

Why: Are you waiting for Monday? Or maybe January 1st.

Are you guilty? I have been.

There's no magic day to make a change. You've got to add action to that desire.

It's easy to put off change. We want a quick solution. Change can be painful. New workouts make you sore. Taking a new course in life can cause you to make choices with emotional consequences. However, without that action, you can bet you'll remain exactly where you are today.

One simple step to get your started begins by writing it down. Maybe more than once. Stick it to your refrigerator. Write it on your mirror. Put a card in your wallet. Put it in a frame by your bed. There's something about committing the words to paper that feels like a contract or promise to yourself.

When you see it over and over throughout your day, you're more likely to think about it as you make decisions. This will keep you focused and moving down the right path.

Don't waste the next 30 days waiting for the right day to begin your journey. We're only given one life, quit waiting for the perfect day to start living the one you dream of.

ABOUT CHELLIE: Chellie W. Phillips, lives a double life. She's the award winning author of When In Doubt, Delete It! and the creator of Successfully Ever After, a personal career branding program designed to land you in the interview seat of your dream job. She's also the Vice President of Communications and Public Relations for Coweta Fayette Electric Membership Corporation. She's an active member of the community, serving on the board of Elevate Coweta Students and the Coweta Community Foundation. She has spent over 20 years in corporate public relations, mentored over 700 college women as they prepared to enter the workforce and has been a speaker at the national level. She's an advocate for ambitious (no that's not a dirty word) women who are motivated to succeed..

FOLLOW UP: THE FORTUNE IS IN THE FOLLOW UP - LAURA LEIST

The Habit: Follow Up: The Fortune is in the Follow Up

By Laura Leist, CPO®, MOS® - Speaker, Productivity
Specialist and Founder of Eliminate Chaos

Why: An excellent system for follow up, whether at work or home, is a habit I've used for 20 years in my business and even longer in my personal life. By systematizing the follow up I do with our clients, it has proven that "the fortune is in the follow-up."

I use two systems for follow up in my office. The first system I use is a specific way I set custom Outlook reminders when I send emails or reply to an email. These emails are also attached as history items to our CRM

(Customer Relationship Management) system, which is the second system we use.

Using a CRM, we can identify leads that may turn into opportunities for prospective clients and opportunities we have with existing clients.

One of the first things I do every day when I get to the office is to quickly review my email reminders to see if there is an email I need to follow up on. Here's how my system works and how this can help you at work. When I send an email to someone that is time-sensitive; meaning I need a response by a specific date, or if I am sending a proposal to a potential client, or maybe I am following up with a client to do more work on their project, I always set a custom follow up flag in my Outlook email. I do this before I send the email, that is the key. By doing this, on the given day, I set the follow-up flag for, I will see a reminder in my Outlook. The reminder is just like a meeting reminder, but instead, it has an envelope icon in front of it. When I look at all the reminders when I get to work, I can open each email from the reminder area to see if I have heard from that individual. If I have, then I can either delete the email or dismiss the reminder, which will leave a copy of the email in my outbox. If, on the other hand, the individual I sent the email to has not responded, it's the perfect opportunity for me to respond to that individual and check-in with them.

Sometimes I must send another email to this person several times, each time setting a new custom follow up flag. At some point, if I never hear back, I must determine if it is worth my time to continue the follow-up. What I find is that people get busy, and they meant to respond, but the timing isn't right for them, or the email got buried in their inbox. By doing the follow-up, I may have reached them at a better time, or at least my email is near the top of their inbox again.

The success rate I have had by using my email follow up system in this way has likely earned *Eliminate Chaos* hundreds of thousands of dollars over the years I've been in business, and people thank me for following up with them because they say that today, no one does this.

My follow up system using our CRM looks a bit different. I schedule weekly time to review our current leads and open opportunities. When I enter the activity to follow up on a lead or opportunity, I typically set the activity for me to do on a Tuesday morning, because at some point in my career, I heard this was the best day to do follow up. I either make my phone calls, send an email, or a text - depending on the preferred method of contact, which I track, so I know how someone likes to be communicated with. If I send an email, I again use the custom follow up flag setting so that it will show up in my Outlook, since my Outlook and our CRM are tied together. If I am unable to reach the individual as planned, I set another activity to remind me to check in with them again at some point in the future. Sometimes when I do the follow-up, and I reach someone in person, they tell me now is not a good time, but to check back in with them at a particular date in the future, which I then schedule in our CRM and I do the follow up again at that time.

By using these two systems at work, not only do I have all of my information in one place, but our entire team also has access to the same leads and opportunities in our CRM and they can also see the email history I've had with this individual, should I ever turn the follow up over to someone else, like a sales professional or another employee.

In my personal life, I still use custom email reminders when it makes sense, but I also have two hanging files in my daily action center. One is labeled "Follow Up," and for some of our clients where I've implemented this, they call it "Pending." In this folder, I place items that I've acted on but am waiting for someone else to complete the next step. In other words, there is nothing else I can do until I hear back from this person. Some examples of this might be when I send back a copy of a claim form to insurance for Chaos, my Bernese Mountain dog, to get reimbursement for his vet visit or medicine. Or maybe I place documents I've sent to others for when I've moved, and I need written confirmation that they've updated our address or name change on specific documents. There are so many different things I use this folder for, and every month, I review it to see what has been completed and can remove from the folder and what I still need to follow up on.

I hope that my systems I use at work and in my personal life will give you some ideas that you can implement so that you can also find the fortune in your follow up.

The Un-Habit: Not Responding to e-mail and voicemail in a timely fashion

WHY: When you don't respond to e-mail or voicemail in a timely fashion, it not only frustrates the individual that has reached out to you, but it also does not make you look professional. Without knowing it, you may also be giving someone the impression that you don't care, don't respect their time, or are not interested in them.

Of course, this may not be how you see it at all or feel about it, but you never know how your lack of response - especially when you requested information, it was provided to you, and you don't respond will form an impression of you on the other person.

I get it, everyone is busy, but can't you afford at least one or two minutes to return a voicemail or send a quick e-mail response? If you are too busy to respond, you can always say something like, "I wanted to acknowledge that I received your e-mail, and I will get back to you by X date." Where the "X" stands for a date that you can respond by. Sometimes people need to know that you've received their e-mail or voicemail and that it has not found its way to the black hole. I know that I certainly appreciate this gesture when someone does this for me.

Countless times, I've had clients and potential clients thank me just for responding. Sometimes they even comment on how quickly I or someone else from our team responds. I sometimes laugh because this comes naturally to me and makes me wonder why more people don't do it. I know how much people appreciate communication because they tell me this.

If you are someone that doesn't always respond or respond in a timely fashion, see how you can up your game and watch the reaction you receive. I think you may also find that people want to do business with people they know will respond and that their needs are being taken care of.

About Laura: Since launching Eliminate Chaos in 2000, Laura Leist has walked her own talk about getting more done to allow "More Time for Life®." A poster child for getting much accomplished, this self-described over-achiever and award-winning entrepreneur has grown what was once a one-woman show into a thriving business. She has written 13 books, including:

Eliminate the Chaos at Work: 25 Techniques to Increase Productivity (Wiley)

Eliminate Chaos: The 10-Step Process to Organize Your Home & Life (Sasquatch Books)

Increase Your Productivity Using Microsoft® Outlook

OneNote: Data at Your Fingertips, Anytime, Anywhere and from Any Device

Today Eliminate Chaos operates three divisions – Productivity and IT Consulting, Residential Organizing and Relocation Services, and Speaking.

Appreciative clients include CEOs of multi-billion-dollar corporations, paper-and-systems-fatigued law offices, high-profile authors, speakers, athletes and media personalities, solopreneurs, and divas of domesticity. Though they come from all walks of life and work, they all share a universal need to invest in professional help to escape the clutter, disorganization and lack of productivity that slows them down, steals valuable time from their lives, and puts a crimp on their upside earning potential.

Creating Order Out of Chaos So Clients Find What They Need Fast

Clients come to Laura overwhelmed by technology tools and the steep learning curves associated with making the most of them. Laura consults with clients about their business processes and creates custom productivity systems. As a result, clients gain control and mastery over mobile devices, customer relationship management tools, and file sharing systems that save them valuable time and make life a whole lot easier. For those for whom technology tools were once a challenge, this is cause for celebration.

. . .

Success by the Numbers

After almost two decades of growth, Laura has built a company that is proud to have served thousands of clients. They sing praises about how the power of organization, systems, processes, and logical workflow has changed their lives, advanced their careers, and saved hours of frustration. Along the way, Laura has:

• Presented over 500 seminars and keynotes about business productivity and organization in the workplace and at home.

• Served in four board positions for the National Association of Productivity and Organizing Professionals (NAPO), including the top position of president. In addition, she earned the NAPO Shining Star Award, recognizing her vision, project management, leadership in redesigning the NAPO website.

• Been among the first in the nation to earn the prestigious Certified Professional Organizer, CPO® designation.

• Earned a degree in Management Information Systems from Washington State University and a certificate in Software Product Management the University of Washington.

• Earned recognition in 2001 as one of the 40 business executives under 40 years of age making a difference in the community by the Puget Sound Business Journal.

Laura came by her organizing genius out of necessity.

From a very early age, Laura made sure her Mom – a visually impaired, music teacher -- could find what she needed when she needed it. These early acts of service and love built a strong appreciation for form, function and order. Today she and her team orchestrate beautiful and elegant organizing systems, processes, and workflows to create symphonies of order, productivity, and more.

Laura loves to travel, and her favorite destination is Hawaii. She and her husband Robert were married on the well-ordered date of 9-10-11 in Maui.

Laura and Rob share their home with "Chaos" – a Bernese Mountain Dog – and Laura jokes that he is the only Chaos she won't "eliminate."

Laura will tell you that it's the treasured moments in life that matter most; not the "stuff."

30

WALK AND EMOTIONALLY VISUALIZE YOUR DESIRES AND AFFIRMATIONS AT LEAST ONCE A DAY - SARA DUDLEY CAMPBELL

The Habit: Walk and Emotionally visualize your desires and affirmations at least once a day

By Sara Dudley Campbell - wife, mother of 2, and Realtor at Zeitlin-Sotheby's International Realty in Nashville, TN

Why: Metaphysics has proven the universe doesn't know the difference between a thought and reality. Use it to your advantage.

In my darkest times, I truly believed I was cursed. It seemed as though most everything that could go wrong did go wrong. I finally gave up "efforting," and began seeking a spiritual path different than the traditional Southern Baptist path with which my family raised me. It is there, where I found my faith and redemption.

After reading many books, and listening to many speakers, I learned they were all saying the same thing – hope is a beggar. The Universe/God/Source Energy sees right through hope. Faith truly believes that what you want has come to pass – you just haven't intersected with it yet in your reality. Mark 11:24 says, "All things whatsoever ye pray and ask for, believe that ye have received them, and ye shall receive them."

Almost every day, I walk for 50 minutes on a neighborhood route. This walk is sacred to me, and I have manifested many things on these magical walks. For the first 20 minutes, I say all the things I am grateful for that are already in my life. This accomplishes two things. First, why would God give me more if I'm not grateful for what I already have? And, two, by the time I'm finished, I'm already in the mindset that I can have my heart's desires.

For the remaining 30 minutes, I say out loud (yes, my neighbors can see me talking to myself) that I am grateful for having all the things (situations, feelings, people, etc.) I want as if I already have them. As an example, I say, "I am so grateful and excited that I have two closings a month worth "x" amount of dollars! It is so fun to be so abundant, and I am so thankful." Another statement I make often is, "I am so happy about all the exciting and new opportunities that I am presented with – it's so fun saying "yes" to all of them!"

I go into great detail about the things or situations I desire. For instance, I have a dream lake house in my mind. I say out loud, "I am so happy about the lake house we are building! The windows all across the back of it are so beautiful, there are beautiful plants all over the deck, and my favorite feature is the conversation pit in the den with the forest green and navy pillows. Our dock has plenty of bench seating, a built-in cooler, a grill, some covered space, and a slide. The kids have so much fun bringing their friends."

I do this for 30 solid minutes, going through many emotions of joy, happy tears, excitement, peace, and confidence. I have manifested many things/opportunities/situations on these walks, and I am getting better at it each day. I also request an unusual animal experience on these walks, and many friends can attest to the fact that I have those experiences more often than not.

This habit is one I look forward to daily because I have seen the results of my efforts. It is also a sure-fire way to turn a bad mood, or a bleak day, around very quickly.

The Un-Habit: Quit drinking soda

Why: There are no benefits from drinking soda, and there are over a dozen health risks. The amount of sugar is astronomical. Excess sugar leads to diabetes, heart disease, obesity, and it feeds cancer. The caramel coloring has also been linked to cancer. The cans are lined with BPA, which is a hormone disruptor that is affected by developing teens dramatically. Soda also depletes your minerals, changes your metabolism, and is linked to Non-Alcoholic Fatty Liver Disease. I also feel very unsophisticated drinking it and wish I could acquire the taste for coffee.

Breaking this habit would change my life by alleviating my worries about those health issues, and I would quickly lose a few pounds that are attributed to my consumption of it. Breaking this habit would also stop the withdrawal headaches when it's been too long since I've had one. I'll be more hydrated, and I won't be at greater risk of cavities or tooth enamel issues. It would be nice to not spend the money on it, and not worry about my "morning soda" when I'm traveling (which is much like that jittery panic when a coffee drinker can't locate their coffee). I don't like that I'm setting a bad example for my kids, even though they are not allowed to drink it. It is my liquid-cigarette when I am stressed, hungry, upset, or in the car, and I will be so glad when I make the decision, once and for all, to put it behind me.

About Sara: Sara Dudley Campbell is a wife, mother of two, and a Realtor with Zeitlin-Sotheby's International Realty in Nashville, TN. She has taken the long way to find the career she loves, having tried many things to get there. She's most proud of her family; and her discovery of the fact that she is more in control of her life than she thought through her habit.

31

FIRST THING WHEN I WAKE UP IN THE MORNING, I SAY THE MODEH ANI (IN HEBREW) - NAOMI BAREKET

The Habit: First thing when I wake up in the morning, I say the Modeh Ani (in Hebrew)

By Naomi Bareket - MBA, NLP Trainer, Author, Speaker

Why: Saying the *MODE ANI*, [*"I give thanks before you, King living and eternal, for You have returned within me my soul with compassion; abundant is Your faithfulness!" (Meaning: G-d's faithfulness in me,)]*, first thing upon waking up in the morning sets the tone for the rest of the day.

Sleep is where one's soul leaves the body.

G-d chose to restore our soul into our body because He believed in us that we were worthy of another day of life to do Tikun Olam – mending and making the world a better place.

Researches show that

1. Your mood in the morning affects your productivity all day. The fact that you appreciate your being alive creates positive thoughts that create a happy, productive day, and peace of mind, and create energy for the day ahead.

2. Having a sense of purpose prolong life

The feeling that you're on a mission. You have a destiny. Your life has meaning.

It gives you confidence for the fact that you are just a being /a chosen being first of all.

3. Feeling a sense of purpose, doing something in service of a cause larger than myself, is one of the most motivating things.

Viktor Frankl "Everything can be taken from a man but one thing: the last of the human freedoms — to choose one's attitude in any given set of circumstances, to choose one's way."

4. People who live with a sense of purpose tend to live longer.

So saying the Modeh Ani reminds you to be grateful and to check on your purpose daily.

Ask yourself every morning, "Am I contributing to the world? 'Am I doing something in service of a cause larger than myself?'"

It brings your consciousness into perspective, that life is a gift with purpose,

and that G-d puts His faith in you that you live the day in the best way possible.

In a book of the standard code of the Jewish law (Shulchan Aruch,) it says, "One should strengthen himself like a lion to get up in the morning to serve his Creator."

A perspective of "I'm on a mission here" is a great boost of motivation, and it improves your focus on the most important things.

It fills in your brain with positive thoughts and helps you overcome the tendency of what neurosciences call 'negativity bias' of the brain.

So when you wake up, and the first thing you realized the blessing of getting another chance to serve others, to have a higher intention for the day and life, then naturally your performances are on the spot/better. You are more likely to live life with no excuses. And focus on living your mission.

And it is like a magical cycle of goodness. Because this realization impacts your perspective to choose to see the good, and when you see more good, your performances and results are better.

So as soon as you open your eyes in the morning, know that your soul came back to you, be thankful, and purposeful. We don't need to wait for Thanksgiving to be thankful for your life. Live it daily!

The Un-Habit: Being a perfectionist

Why: Breaking this Habit of perfectionism will help you loosen up; you would be more flexible and creative. You will gain more opportunities and be daring to take new projects. You will start and complete more tasks. Your self-esteem improves as you won't depend on others to validate you. You will accomplish much more. You will be less stressed and anxious.

You will build better relations, as you will view the people around you in more positivity and be less judgmental. And you will delegate tasks as you would trust others too.

You will fulfill more of your potential as you will compare yourself to yourself rather than to others. Develop appropriate expectations and standards that allow you more freedom and flexibility moving forward. You will have more realistic expectations for yourself; therefore, you will get more things done.

Remember, we are all human beings, better-doing mistakes while doing, then being stuck afraid of making mistakes.

Set small deadlines within the timeline for a given project. Start a project right away, complete it, and revise it later if needed.

Set realistic standards and objectives. Focus on what matters. Focus on the big picture.

Practice delegating more and appreciate what is done.

It reminded me of when I was going to hear a lecture, and the lecturer didn't show up. The person who facilitated the event asked me if I was willing to speak instead. He caught me by surprise. Before the internal dialogue kicks in, and let my perfectionist part tried to distract me, I said, "Sure, with love."

I couldn't skip such an opportunity even if it meant that I wouldn't deliver a perfect lecture. I could easily say, "No way," and came with all kinds of excuses like "I don't have the powerpoint presentation, and my board and markers."

I made him so happy when I said, "sure, with love."

Many approached me afterward, telling me that I was so brave to take the stage out of the blue. They would be too afraid to do it spontaneously themselves had they been asked.

I'm so glad I chose to say yes. I engaged a lot with the audience, and they said it was thought-provoking for them. People who hadn't met me before learned more about me, and if I inspired them, that was fulfilling, as I felt I was here on earth for encouraging others to claim they are true self and fulfill their potential and mission. It was a great moment.

 **ABOUT NAOMI:** Naomi Bareket: MBA, is a Speaker and dynamic Seminar Leader who uses modern techniques and Kabbalistic wisdom to facilitate you to own your power, take charge of your mind, realize your motivator factors, and be in congruence internally and with your team. Bareket is the co-creator of NeuroSUCCESSology™ whereby she offers her broad experience in linguistics, Time Line Therapy®, hypnosis, neuroscience, Kabbalah, and the field of Neuro-Linguistic Programming (NLP) to empower you to create lives of fulfillment.

She has been certified by John Maxwell as a Leadership Coach, Teacher, Trainer, and Speaker, and she is certified by the American Board of NLP to train and certify others as NLP practitioners and masters. Bareket is also the author of THE DEEP SEE: How to See into your Soul and Find Who You Are and Want to Be. She loves to combine business with spiritual work. Therefore, she loves to work with entrepreneurs, business owners, coaches, and speakers. Naomi believes that when you live in alignment with your true self, you can fulfill your life's purpose and live a meaningful life.

32

EVERY DAY, IN THE MIDDLE OF YOUR DAY, TAKE 60 SECONDS TO MAKE A P.I.T. STOP -- IT'S YOUR POWER INFUSION TIME - EVANGELINE COLBERT

The Habit: Every day, in the middle of your day, take 60 seconds to make a P.I.T. Stop -- it's your Power Infusion Time.

By Evangeline Colbert - Victorious Living Coach/Author

Why: In our global society, life is on the go 24/7. We can easily find ourselves entrapped in so much busyness that our thoughts and emotions are always "on." Considering that we have jobs to go to, family care responsibilities, community activities to attend, and need six to eight hours of restful sleep, we may rarely take the opportunity to fully exhale and do something to rejuvenate our spirit.

Making a quick daily P.I.T. Stop for 60 seconds can change that. A P.I.T. Stop is your "Power Infusion Time."

You could look at these short bursts of time as the pit stop that race car drivers make during their hours-long race. They pull over and stop...they stop not only to get tires changed but to refuel their bodies and the car. What if we "pulled over" throughout the day to refuel the most important part of us—our spirit? How much better would life be? I think we'd be much more likely to decrease our defeats and increase our victories.

I have found that in forming the habit of making a P.I.T. Stop, "pulling over" can easily be done in snippets of 60 seconds here and there throughout the day. These P.I.T. stops can be a practical key to your success. During those times, you can pray, take deep breaths, recite a calming Scripture passage or an inspirational quote, reflect on the lyrics of an uplifting song, express gratitude for simple blessings, or something else that restores your soul. And yes, you really can do it in 60 seconds.

Maybe for you, it's important to find ways to infuse the power of God into your life. Psalm 1:3 NLT. shows us that the people who frequently meditate on God's Word "are like trees planted along the riverbank, bearing fruit each season. Their leaves never wither, and they prosper in all they do." If you were to meditate on that particular verse, you could occasionally whisper to yourself throughout the day, "I am like a tree planted near water, always bearing fruit at the right time, never shriveling or unhealthy, always prospering." Change the words if you like, but thinking and speaking this way can firmly establish you for success in every area of your life.

To become more diligent at doing these P.I.T. stops, I set the alarm on my phone to go off at a specific time every day, Sunday-Saturday, to remind me to take just 60 seconds, right at that moment to refuel and restore myself. It doesn't matter whether I'm driving, working at my desk, at the grocery store, or involved in some other activity, I can quickly infuse positive power into my day and, more importantly, my attitude.

I can't tell you the level of peace I've begun to experience and the insights for my life that I've gained just by incorporating this quick habit into my day. It's like answering a call of love when my P.I.T. Stop alarm goes off.

Take time to infuse power into your life. With this quick and simple habit, you'll empower yourself to live to win.

The Un-Habit: Saying negative things about yourself

Why: Many people don't recognize how important and powerful their words are. Their words not only let others know what they think but also their words are vessels filled with the power to change and reframe their world or to keep things the same.

You become what you think about most. Why? Your thoughts will eventually become your spoken words. The things you repeatedly say and hear will eventually influence your actions. Your repeated actions will become your habits. Your habits will always be a clear indicator of your character.

Spoken words program your life either for success or for

defeat. Did you know that our own words can trap us? An old proverb says, "You have been trapped by what you said, ensnared by the words of your mouth."

Typically the more you tell people about your lack, you experience more lack. When you focus on your failures and weaknesses, you begin to see and develop more of them.

When there's self-denigration coming out of your mouth-- putting yourself down and verbally expressing that you're EXPECTING failure or defeat in some way—it can become a self-fulfilling prophecy.

Likewise, there is a language of success. It is a language filled with the power of life. When you let your self-talk and conversations with others habitually reflect life and positivity, it increases your ability to change the direction of your life positively.

Live life being cognizant that your words can ensnare you, but they can also free you. Propose to make it a habit to go through each day speaking words of life, victory, and blessing!

About Evangeline: Evangeline Colbert is an author, speaker, and Hope Coach. She loves seeing people's lives transformed! She teaches her audiences how to use the power of their words and the Word of God to change their circumstances and to live life victoriously.

Her book, "Live to Win! 5 Essentials for Your Victory and Success," is a blueprint for living life like the champion you were created to be. You'll discover powerful strategies that are packed with the wisdom of God. She outlines five essential principles, all based on the promises of God, which become pathways leading to successful living.

She is a Certified Professional Coach and uses the principles found in Live to Win to help her clients live like champions.

She has also written a devotional about overcoming infertility, "A Seed of Hope: God's Promises of Fertility." It is written from the perspective of her personal victory over infertility. Her most recent book is one she co-authored with Angela Williams to give women more hope about their fertility. The title is "Borrowed Hope" and it is the first in a series of books about the struggles of women in the Bible who each overcame infertility.

Evangeline is dedicated to helping others find and maintain hope in the midst of their everyday struggles so that they persevere with confidence and live with a hope-filled focus. If hope, victory, and meaningful results are what you're craving, one of her coaching programs can get you there.

Her highest goal is to help others live their best life, with courage, purpose, and joy!

33

INHALE THE POSITIVE, EXHALE THE NEGATIVE - DIVYA SIEUDARSAN-HARLALL

The Habit: Inhale the positive, Exhale the negative

By Divya Sieudarsan-Harlall - Author/Youtuber/Fulltime Mama

Why: In today's world, women wear so many hats while balancing work, home, relationships, and so much more. While doing this, our emotions sometimes take over and give into the negative self-talk. We give into anger; we give into doubt; we give into being victims of this unfair world. The naysayers' voices seem to become louder in our heads, and anxiety starts to step in. This can all have a crippling effect on our state of mind, which then affects productivity and how you treat others. Instead of thinking you're an amazing super being, you start to doubt your ability and question yourself. You start to become reactive, reacting to every situation or to what people throw at you rather than being proactive. No one wants to go through this, but the truth is it happens, and we need to learn how to cope with this. I hope everyone has a preventative plan and a plan of action for when this downward spiral happens. Do you? Don't worry, I didn't either, or at least I didn't realize I had the tools I needed to combat these emotions and prevent it from escalating in my mind.

When I get angry or anxious, I would take deep breaths in and then release slowly to calm myself down or to not get overly emotional. Basically, slowly let some air out of the balloon, which was about to POP! As I started coping with getting rid of emotions that put me down, I started telling myself to breathe in all the love, all the positive ions, all the support, all the great things that surround me and all that I am grateful for. Then as I breathe out, I release all that pent up emotion, all the anger, all the anxiety, and all the negative feelings that cloud my brain, causing confusion and making me feel like I'm helpless and not capable of getting anything done.

Let's face it. When you tell yourself you cannot get something done, then that's precisely what happens. So, this was working great for me. Whenever I felt derailed, I would breathe in all the positive energy and breathe out the negative feelings. However, I was still reactive. I then decided that at the beginning of each day, I will make some time for myself and breathe in the love, possibilities, and positivity and breathe out limitations, doubt, and negativity.

It didn't stop there. You must always work on improving your method. When I got pregnant, I started doing deep breathing (from my belly, not chest), and I realized if I zoned out, I could truly focus on my breathing or any one particular thing without the background noise in my head. So here's my one habit that helps me kick-start my day and ensure I get the maximum awesomeness from my day; at the beginning of my day, I sit on my bed or the floor, legs crossed, and take deep long belly breaths. I slowly breathe in through the nose, taking in all the gratitude, all the love, and all the positivity possible with a smile on my face (If you don't feel like smiling, by the end of this breathing exercise, you will!).

I even squint a little because I take a big breath in, hold a bit, then very slowly, release through the mouth. I am releasing all the negative thoughts that occupy my mind, body, and soul. Release any uncertainty and doubt. As you are releasing these obstructive elements from your mind, you can feel that space being filled with renewed energy. I do this until I feel fully balanced, recharged, and energized. This habit has kept me leveled and calm in the middle of chaos. I have an eight-month-old, and panicking will not help either of us; he feeds off of my energy. If I'm nervous or anxious, he feels it. I love feeling calm and in control, especially around my child, because he then feels secured. This could be you with clients or anyone around you. When you are calm and in control, the people around you feel more secured and confident in you.

The Un-Habit: Setting "triggers"

Why: One Habit I hope with all my might that you break free from is letting other people's words and actions negatively affect you or provoke you.

We are all responsible for our actions. Therefore, the only one who knows what "triggers" me is me; the same goes with you. We put up that barrier and say if someone does this, then that will set off my "trigger", but why do we do that to ourselves? If I'm angry at person x, who does it affect? Me or them? It's me! I'm the one getting all hot and bothered at this person, using my energy to be mad at them, and they have no idea or interest. They move on, however, we don't just move on; we're mentally invested now. We have to find an outlet to get rid of this anger and we have to mentally heal ourselves again. Is this worth it? Is it worth my time? Is it worth my energy?

Setting triggers is us setting ourselves up for failure. Someone is bound to do things we do not approve of, but that shouldn't affect us and cost us wasted emotions. Everyone has control over their actions and are responsible for those actions and their emotions. Do not let other people kill your vibe or ruin your free-flowing thoughts. This is a tough habit to break, but every time you feel someone is getting into "your space" or "in your head" or "under your skin", setting off a "trigger", keep reminding yourself that you are in charge of your own emotions; you are in charge of your actions. You are not going to rob yourself of your peace of mind and joy just because you aren't happy with the actions of others.

Choose happiness and peace of mind over chaos and anger. Choose yourself.

ABOUT DIVYA: Divya Sieudarsan-Harlall is an award-winning international best-selling author, Youtuber and full time Mama. She has experience on stage, on the mic and on the catwalk. Divya isn't just a pretty smile, she's a highly motivated woman who is dedicated to using her experience as a first time mom to help other moms everywhere through social media especially YouTube.

Divya became an entrepreneur at the age of 22, apart from being a marketing consultant she has vast experience and knowledge in accounting, aviation, customer service, Human Resources, sales, training and management.

Divya has represented her country, Guyana, internationally as Miss India-Guyana 2014.

She has worked with various organizations and volunteers to help make a difference in people's lives. Divya believes that positive energy can overcome hardships that lead to a happier, healthier and wealthier life.

34

CHOOSE TO COME FROM A PLACE OF LOVE INSTEAD OF FEAR EVERY SINGLE DAY - NATALIE SUSI

The Habit: Choose to come from a place of love instead of fear every single day

By Natalie Susi - Teacher, Writer, Entrepreneur

Why: Your life is a culmination of the decisions you make every single day to get you to where you are right now. In every one of these circumstances, you have a choice to react from a place of fear or take action from a place of love.

The choice is simple, but it is not always easy.

The ego triggers fear-based thoughts, words, and emotions. They sound like, "I'm so angry because this person did XYZ thing to me."

Or, "I feel so depressed because I didn't get the XYZ result that I wanted." This way of thinking creates barriers, stagnation, and drama, and it repels the people and opportunities that could help you manifest your desires.

Whenever I have to make a decision, I ask myself these questions: "Am I coming from a place of love or fear right now?" If I am feeling frustrated, sad, or anxious, I ask, "What am I afraid of here?"

And then, "How can I change my actions to reflect a heart-centered, non-judgmental, love-based that supports myself and others?

Consistently choosing love over fear takes practice, and it doesn't always feel comfortable. It is a life-changing mindset shift.

When you choose to love, you make it safe for others to choose love too. You become the person who inspires honesty, vulnerability, and conscious conversations. You make it possible for people to learn, grow, and create from an authentic, genuine place that serves both the individual and the group.

This little shift in awareness creates a big shift in the collective consciousness and makes a significant positive impact on our planet.

The Un-Habit: Stop negative thinking in its tracks

Why: All creation starts with a thought. Positive thoughts generally lead to positive outcomes. Negative thoughts lead to negative outcomes. We are very powerful, and we can manifest whatever we want in our lives. The best way to start living a life that is in alignment with your vision and your desires is to start consciously getting into the habit of shifting your negative mindset to a positive one. Whenever I think of a negative thought, I do a little trick that I call "turning it over." I challenge myself to turn it into a positive thought even if that doesn't feel real or accurate at first. I begin to say the positive version of the original negative thought until it feels more and more possible. Eventually, I will start to see things show up in my reality that indicates a situation has started to shift. This takes time, practice, and trust in yourself and the power of our thoughts and our energy. Once you commit to doing this process over and over again, you start to train your brain into "turning over" the negative thoughts and shifting them into positive ones, and this becomes your new habit and your new normal.

About Natalie: Natalie Susi is a teacher by heart, a writer by trade, and an entrepreneur by choice.

Natalie began her entrepreneurial journey in 2009 when she recognized a gap in the marketplace for all-natural, low-calorie cocktail mixers. She founded Bare Organic Mixers and sold the company in 2014. She and Bare were featured in some notable outlets to include: The LA Times, People Magazine, Bravo, Pacific Magazine (Top 30 Entrepreneurs Under 30), and Forbes.com (Top 10 Female Entrepreneurs to Watch in SD).

In the process of building a startup, and in an attempt to consciously navigate the life and business challenges that first-time entrepreneurs often face, Natalie became fascinated with the study of human behavior and psychology and spiritual and personal development principles like how to overcome limiting beliefs, how to align mind, body, and spirit, and how to get out of what she calls a "ditch moment."

After selling the company, Natalie combined her educational background as a teacher and her experience as an entrepreneur to provide personal development coaching and consulting to individuals, businesses, and creative entrepreneurs. She developed a step-by-step program called "Creating a Conscious Culture" that can be utilized in corporate, academic, or personal one-on-one settings to guide people through a process of self-reflection, self-discovery, and self-improvement.

She is also a professor at the University of California, San Diego where she teaches a course called "The Pursuit of Happiness."

Natalie's ultimate goal is to be a part of creating a world where everyone has access to the principles and tools that will guide them in engaging in conscious reflection, communication, and creation, so they can learn, grow, and transform and create a ripple effect of positive impact for themselves, their loved ones, and the world.

35

SHARE YOUR SMILE - IRENE ZAMARO

The Habit: Share Your Smile

By Irene Zamaro - Founder of Tradeshows Today

Why: Did you know that smiling at others, even a complete stranger, can brighten up their day? Someone could be having a tough time and just that small gesture could turn their entire day around. Smiling is an action of love and many people out there need to be assured that someone cares for them. It's one of the most priceless gifts that you ever give to anyone, it's so simple to share and it doesn't cost a dime!

I believe in positive energy and passing that along to the people I meet. This positive energy creates a connection with people and leads to opportunities. By opening hearts, you can open doors. The smile is the best way to project a positive mindset and that simple gesture can spread this positivity to people that didn't even realize they needed it.

I have been approached so many times by strangers that have told me they don't normally talk to people they don't know but something drew them to me. I truly believe my positive energy creates a connection that allows people to be genuine and positive. It allows a real conversation in a world where everyone protects and guards their true self. It can be so nice to find a positive oasis in the artificial online world.

I enjoy sharing my smile. It warms my heart to see how such a simple reflex to a perfect stranger can brighten someone's spirt effortlessly. I enjoy the connection it makes to learn about someone that would have never taken the time of day otherwise to talk to you. It can break down those walls we all put up and allow you to see a completely different world. My reward in return is seeing true people, hearing their honest stories and appreciating the struggles we all go through day to day. We all have problems, not matter how big or small and it's reassuring to know we are not alone.

We live in a world of apps, texting and online communications. The true networking connection is made when you let your guard down and share your smile. You never know how much of a difference you could be making in to someone life in that moment.

The Un-Habit: Understanding our thoughts

Why: It is so easy for us to get caught up in our own thoughts. It's easy to lose ourselves in this chaotic life and not even realize it. So many times, you get stuck in a "rut," a "pattern" or start going through the motions. We look at where you want to be in the next month, the next year or longer. Goals are essential, but we also need to stay in the moment and appreciate where we are right now. That negative rut creates a negative mindset and takes away from the happiness of the moment. What good is the result if we don't appreciate it the entire journey, the good and the bad.

I think life should be about touching the lives of people around us and making a difference. Appreciating people for who they are and going out of your way to help others regardless of our differences. What fun would it be if we all thought the same? So many people pass us day to day, each one has a story, each one can impact our lives if we are open to the opportunity.

You might have the best plan for yourself, and by not engaging in the moment, miss out on your true direction and an excellent opportunity. Love where you are and love what you have at that moment. Strive for your goals and success but not overlook the opportunities that present themselves to you each day. You never know where the road ends, so enjoy every curve!

About Irene: Throughout my life, I have worked a 9 to 5 job and played it safe. I was a regular mom with three

wonderful children that I love.
Several years ago, my two youngest children began to lose their sight. They developed a disease that has since resulted in both becoming legally blind. This broke my heart as a mother but watching their resiliency and ability to enjoy their lives despite this hardship has opened my eyes and inspired me.

I have always had an enthusiasm for meeting people and developing relationships with positive individuals. Inspired by my children, I've stopped holding myself back and took the risk to pursue my true professional joy. I love trade shows, networking events and learning new skills. I offer my enthusiasm to companies to pump energy into their exciting new products and services. I can take an ordinary booth at a trade show and increase traffic by 100%. My passion has taken me across the United States and ventured to foreign countries.

Currently my passion has taken me too higher levels in my career and have become an ambassador for these multiple companies (Craig Shelly, Savvy Wellness, Kula Brands and Clar8ty).

MY true passion is working with people.

Recently I have tried to share my story in a way that helps others express their fears and frustrations. I open doors and hearts with my unique energy and leaving people feeling great after interacting with me. I get the chance, through my experience, to re-introduce them to the dreams that had been forgotten or put on the shelf to build dust.

My unique gift of being open and sharing allows me to help give back to charities. One being, City of Hope, that saved by youngest son at stage four cancer. This inspired me to take charge in fighting for a cure for my two adult kids and their deteriorating eye site. I have take the challenges that life has thrown and me and my family and used it as a positive inspiration to drive toward success and believe anything is possible.

36

BECOME THE BEST VERSION OF YOU RELATIONAL VS. TRANSACTIONAL - LEA WOODFORD

The Habit: Become the Best Version of You Relational Vs. Transactional

By Lea Woodford - CEO of SmartFem Media Group

Why: Being an entrepreneur isn't easy, as it requires a lot of work and commitment. However, it can be a lot easier if you do your homework upfront. Having a positive mindset and willingness to be flexible will prepare you for the entrepreneurial journey. When you focus on serving others first, the money will not only come, but other aspects of your life will flourish.

Passion, Purpose, and Skill Set Intersection: We have all heard that you must follow your passion to become successful, and that is partially true. To grow your business, you must also have a purpose and the appropriate skill sets. Your purpose is what will keep you going even when the fun is gone, and it begins to get hard. Your "Why" and or "Purpose must be bigger than your excuses. You must also be willing to learn new skill sets. In today's fast-paced technological world, things change at warp speed, and what worked last year may not now.

What is your superpower? What value do you provide that makes you and your company the best solution to your customer? When you can demonstrate your value up front and show your potential customers that you can solve their problems, they will buy from you.

Understanding who your target demographic is and their challenges will go a long way to build your business. So many business owners try to sell their wares without first having clarity on who their potential customers are and what their issues are. With so many options these days, it is important to know who you serve, how you serve, and what problem you solve.

Quit Selling: The consumer has changed with technology, and so must your sales approach. The old adage is true... "People buy from people they know like and trust." Instead of trying to convince and pitch your potential customers, why not provide value upfront. People are savvy and know if a gimmick or a slick advertisement is coming. The reason most people struggle is because they forget to build a relationship first, instead of trying to make the sale, why not make a connection.

Emotional Connection: People want to be seen and

heard. Why not have a conversation and ask people what they want? Active listening will go a long way to forge a strong relationship and enable you to understand the needs of your potential customer. In the immortal words of Maya Angelou, "People may not remember what you say, but they will remember how you made them feel." To solve a problem, you must first know what it is. When your customer knows you are relational and not transactional, they will become customers for life.

Invest in becoming the very best version of you as it will positively impact all aspects of your life, including your business. People are emotional buyers, so why not make it your life's mission. When you live to serve others and provide value, your customers will stay with you, and you will never have a competitor.

The Un-Habit: Quit being transactional

Why: Transactional people struggle in all aspects of their life such as health, happiness, relationships, and of course, business. They do not look to serve as they are only interested in what they can get. They are skeptical, selfish, and unhappy. They struggle in all aspects of their lives. They struggle financially and are always looking to make a quick sale at any cost.

We all know transactional people who are self-serving and looking only to benefit themselves. These people have situational happiness meaning that they can only be happy when they get what they want. These brief stints of happiness are always short-lived.

When it comes to life or business, we must invest in becoming the best version of ourselves. To have a friend, you must be a friend. When you start becoming the best version of yourself and become relational vs. transactional, your entire life will shift. You will be able to cultivate self-esteem, happiness, and meaningful relationships. The benefits to your business will skyrocket as you will have the ability to have life-long customers instead of a one and done sale.

In conclusion, becoming the best version of you will transcend all aspects of your life i.e., health, wealth, happiness, and security. Imagine starting every day with a smile and a sense of wonder and gratitude instead of frustration and fear. You may not be able to change other people, but when you change how you show up and how you react the world changes in return. Isn't it time that you became who you were meant to be?

 **About Lea:** Lea Woodford is the Chief Executive Officer and founder of the SmartFem Media Group, a full service digital marketing and advertising company. SmartFem was created as a result of her many years as a publicist, columnist and as a Radio & TV Personality. Lea has extensive experience as a business consultant and entrepreneur but decided the only way she could make a difference for women was to create her own magazine that bridges the online community with the local community. Her passion is in connecting people. In fact

Lea is often called " the connector " due to her extensive network. Her show SmartFem TV is part of the C-Suite Network out of New York and is magazine helps create opportunities for interns and graduates from ASU's Walter being featured in the major airports and luxury hotels. Her award-winning magazine SmartFem has been recognized by the Business Journal as well as other members of Arizona Legislation for her work with women and the non-profit community. Lea is passionate about working with young professionals and ensures that SmartFem Cronkite School.

When it comes to speaking, Lea is a breath of fresh air, focusing on leadership, innovation and change to drive business. Her inspirational stories and humor will engage audiences to start thinking bigger. Lea speaks from experience as she shares her stories on making her online magazine into a full service digital marketing and advertising company. She encourages her audience to think bigger and bolder about their own business. Lea motivates her audience in the same manner she motivates her team, "find your voice." Lea shares her ups and downs as well as her successes and failures – to give your audience a fresh perspective on marketing, leadership, innovation and customer service.

An online marketing, and social media expert, Lea shares the latest trends to help companies move to the next level in the ever changing digital space. Lea is an expert and a top speaker. She walks her talk. She will impart valuable information in a fun and entertaining way and will leave your audience wanting more.

37

SEE THRU THE EYES OF LOVE - SYLVIA CHAVEZ

The Habit: See thru the eyes of love

By Sylvia Chavez - America's Love Queen

Why: "When you change the way you look at things, the things you look at change."

The first time I heard Wayne Dyer saying that phrase, my whole universe changed. I already had started feeling that the more appreciation I have for everything around me, the happier I felt, and at the same time, the more I showed that happiness to the world, the more the world would give me back their love.

And one day I felt the Magic, I saw every single thing around me with The Eyes Of Love, I even remember my senses felt different, I could appreciate the different smells, the different colors, tastes, even a simple cup of coffee shared with the person I love could become the most exquisite drink. That moment I realized that it was up to me to be happy. That was the day I knew that I could create a life full of love and abundance, by seeing everything with The Eyes Of Love.

This is the story of Sharon. I love the tea on Sharon's Store, so every morning I would go there to get it, to my unpleasant surprise, every day her mood and attitude towards all the clients were very rude. I used to get so upset about her that after a week, I decided to forget about my favorite tea.

Some days went by, and I couldn't stop thinking about Sharon, what if she was going through a bad situation? What if she was going through pain and misfortune? So, I decided to see her with the eyes of love and went back to her store.

That morning as soon as I got to the store I looked at Sharon, and with my biggest possible smile I said to her: "Good Morning, How are you?" to what she answered: "What do you want?"

You can only imagine how I felt. But I was decided, no matter what, I would keep trying.

The same scenario happened for another week until one day, something shifted. She started smiling at me, we would chat about our kids, we became friends, and later on, I found out that she was a single mother with two kids, one of them suffering from a very painful chronic disease. Now, we hug every morning when we say goodbye. We touch each other's lives, and we both look at each other with love and appreciation.

You attract who you are. If you see others with the eyes of love, that is what you are going to receive. And it all starts with your decision, every single day, you can decide how you are going to see the world, to your friends, to your loved ones and even to strangers. You are a mirror of what you see; now you can choose, how would you like to see yourself through the way you look at others?

The Un-Habit: Seeing thru the eyes of judgment

Why: We have an opinion about almost anything and everybody we see, it's an instant judgment: "I like it" or "I don't like it" is the first thought we have, and some things (the least) are neutral. Most of the time, that "judgement" comes from our belief system, even from our subconscious. Our values, the religion we belong to, everything we learn from our parents, previous generations, and even our teachers and friends. And how about the media? The radio, the songs, the tv, facebook, etc., etc.

Emma was a client of mine; she wanted to find the love of her life. The first thing she did was a big list of all the attributes this man needed to have to be "the one" for her. After a while, she met a very nice guy, respectful, good looking, and considerate. He checked many of the "must-have attributes" for the "perfect man description."

But, all of that wasn't enough for Emma, she would judge every single thing that was missing, the restaurant he picked was not good enough for her, the Xmas gift was not expensive enough, she would judge every single act of love from him, and most of the times they would end up the night arguing about her expectations not being met by him.

After a couple of months the relationship ended, he couldn't take so much criticism from her, it was too painful, no matter how hard he tried, he was never good enough.

What do you think it could've happened if instead of the eyes of judgment, Emma could've seen him through the eyes of love and acceptance?

When you judge others, you miss the opportunity of enjoying every good thing that a person has to share. You miss the chance to learn and grow out of that new relationship. You miss the opportunity to take that relationship to a higher and deeper level of connection.

When you see through the eyes of judgment, you are mirroring the worst of you on others. You cut the endless possibilities that a new relationship can bring into your life in many capacities. It is a lose-lose situation.

 **About Sylvia:** Passionate about helping people discover their excellence in love, Sylvia "America's Love Queen " Chavez has dedicated the majority of her life to guiding women. She is an expert in creating a Vision and the

right direction to make that vision a reality. Her entire professional life has led her to make a huge impact on the world.

Thru her program called H.E.R. she teaches her clients how to Heal, Empower and Redesign the relationship with all the areas of their lives as she believes that a broken heart is the root of a disempowering life; a life where one builds an existence based on scarcity and fear, and success is very hard or impossible to accomplished.

Sylvia is a member of Stegela Success Mastery's Leadership, San Diego's largest mastermind, and coaching program. She has been a columnist for "Life by Design Magazine" for 2 years.

Born in Columbus, Georgia and raised in Buenos Aires, Argentina Sylvia Chavez, a Proud Latina moved to Paradise San Diego (as she calls it) 5 years ago.

She is an Exceptional Love Coach, Mentor, and International Speaker.

She has published her own book "131 Keys to Love" in 2019 and she is also one of the featured authors for the books: "Letters to Me: Life Lessons I wish I knew" by Aunt Mary Hang and "Reach your Greatness" by James Malinchak. Recently, Sylvia has started her own Podcast: "Let's Talk about Love"

Sylvia is a Happy Mom of 5 kids from 13 to 35 years old and a recent grandma who enjoys sharing quality time with her husband and loved ones. She loves walking on the beach and breath that peaceful and endless feeling of gratitude and happiness. She is also a singer and shares her passion with her husband, Alejandro, a recognized San Diego Musician.

Sylvia considers herself a Service Person, she strongly believes in leaving a legacy in this world by empowering women all over the world. Her heart is touched by their stories and all she can see in them is the infinite possibilities of success. She is a Heart-Centered Coach Giving Back the Power to those who lost it in their way to surviving life.

"America's Love Queen", Sylvia has touched the lives of hundreds of men and women participating in her 1:1 Coaching, Groups and Workshops overseas and domestic, both in English and in Spanish.

Along the way, Sylvia has discovered how to envision and embrace her own excellence thereby giving her an opportunity to share her dreams and passion of helping people around the world. She loves sharing her expertise so others can discover their essence and make the impact they want to make.

WEARING FAITH EVERYDAY - RUTH YOUNG-LOAEZA

The Habit: Wearing Faith Everyday

By Ruth Young-Loaeza - CEO & Founder Genius On Development

Why: How can a maid go from cleaning houses for 24 years to becoming an inventor and having a patent granted? By wearing faith every day! How can a woman get out of a very violent domestic relationship and barely make it out alive? By wearing faith every day! How can a woman overcome the terrible experience of being raped at the age of 14? By wearing faith every day!

Indeed, believing and living this principle of wearing faith every day has brought an understanding of the importance of giving my self to God and also practicing the difficult task of trusting that He will take care of me. This habit can be difficult because of my lack of faith, not because God can't take care of me. ask your self: Do you challenge your faith?

I will share how I got to the point where the struggle was so much in my life that I just gave out and started wearing faith every day a hundred percent of the time (or at least I tried not to forget that there is only so much I can control and that there is a higher that is in charge of everything). I have goals and giving up for me means that I get down on my knees, lift up my hands and give it to God. Ask yourself: When you can't go on and feel giving up, do you recognize that there is a higher power that can take care of your struggles, or do you into the hole defeated?

As a victim of rape, I went through a period of denial by pretending that nothing had happened to me---but feeling completely worthless. That's how I ended up getting involved in a violent domestic relationship with my children's father, a man 18 years older than me. I lived with him in this abusive situation for eight years, starting when I was only 15. In the last episode of violence, he pretty much gave the choice to live or die by telling me that if I called the cops I would die, but if I didn't call I would be OK. While this was taking place, he had the phone cord wrapped around my neck. Needless to say, that was a no-brainer---I wanted to live, I was only 23 years old. Ask yourself: If you happened to be in an abusive situation, what would it take for you to see the gravity of it?

It was then that I finally realized I had to get out of there before becoming another statistic. I basically escaped with my three children, carrying three suitcases full of my children's clothing and diapers. I then went to a shelter for abused women where I happened to find more abuse. It was wearing faith that took me out of that sick relationship. Ask yourself: When things get worse do you get intimidated or do you seek to come out triumphant?

But once again, faith carried me over throughout those horrible months of living in that small hell town (as I called it). After several weeks of staying at the shelter, I started working my way out and I got a small apartment, bought myself a car, and was able to move away from that toxic environment. By faith is that one can see the light trough the darkest hours! Ask yourself: Are you looking for the light at the end of the tunnel or are you too afraid to move and because of that, you remain in darkness?

Fast forward about ten years later, by which time I had a very stable life. I met the man who's now my husband and we pretty much lived a decent life, until one day I was in a car accident that left me unable to moved and kept me in bed for a couple of months and couldn't work either. This event put us through so much stress that my husband lost his job too, and we ended up homeless, sleeping in his car with our three dogs. It is now that I understand WHY God allowed a tragedy like that to be a part of my life. Ask yourself: Is it worth to have faith and believe that what you are going through will simply make you stronger?

Before this unfortunate event I was a workaholic, but never had time to spend it working on the many ideas I had come up within the many years while working cleaning houses. Time, where does it, go? Ask yourself: Are you redeeming your time wisely?

I believe in God and practice my faith, but I often found myself asking Him to show me what was my talent or the purpose of my life, and how I could leave my mark in this world The funny thing is that it was useless to ask because I wasn't listening or actually even expecting to get the answer anyway. Ask yourself: Are sabotaging yourself the same way I did for many years by asking and answering your own questions?

I had always known that I wanted to have an impact on people's lives, but I was too busy with life... I wasn't listening to what God had to say nor taking the time to receive what He had in store for me. I care for serving and helping others; that's why I have volunteered for the last 18 years of my life. Even during the time that I was homeless, I find it suiting to serve as a volunteer. But I was like the Martha in The Bible busy, busy, but not on the most important task... which was listening to the voice that is the source of faith. Ask yourself: Are you asking and actually paying attention to hear the answer?

But it wasn't enough for me; I wanted more. It wasn't until I was unable to work because of that car accident that I found my creative gifts, and after that, I had all of the time in the world to do something I truly enjoyed and loved. Thanks to what I thought was a tragic event in my life, I discovered that I can create and innovate products that people use each and every day. I have always been resourceful, and as a single mother I couldn't wait for someone else to come and fix whatever was broken at home, so I fixed most of it myself. As of today, I thank God for my husband now he takes care of all of that.

We finally got back on our feet after a few years of being homeless, and both of us are truly grateful to God because of this experience we learned to wear faith every day. I constantly remind myself that everything truly happens for a reason. My mindset is now to remember God is the source of my strength and faith. That's how I live my life, and I am eager to see what he has for me every new day.

The Un-Habit: STOP WORRYING!

Why: I am a practical person, and that's why I will ask you to ask yourself the following questions. Can you unbreak a broken glass? No, you can't! Can you unsay something you said? No, you can't! Can you change the weather? No, you can't! Can you predict the future? No, you can't!

I can ask a dozen silly or rhetorical questions with the hope I make my point clear, but I am sure you get the point. The same principle can be applied when you start getting worried. Getting worried takes a tremendous amount of energy; there is a lot of data that supports the fact that this behavior has a very negative impact on all aspects of one's life.

The adverse effects can be seen physically, mentally, emotionally, spiritually and the list goes on. I learned this after suffering severe migraine headaches and the devastating effects in my own life. I finally learned that it isn't worth worrying about the things that can't be fixed. I'm still working on this habit, but so far it has paid off tremendously—I am so much happier and healthier than I was in my previous years. My relationship with my husband has improved greatly, too.

I read that faith without works is dead faith, so I do just what I'm capable of doing, and I let God do what He is supposed to do. I am now investing all of my efforts into doing positive thinking, and I no longer waste much of my energy in getting worry.

About Ruth: Ruth Young-Loaeza is a small business owner, entrepreneur, and inventor. After recuperating from a car accident that left her and her husband homeless and unable to work, she started creating drawings and prototypes of the many products and ideas she had come up with while she was cleaning houses.

Her journey began after she entered an invention competition. She flew to New York with $50 in her pocket and slept in the rental car, but the next day at the competition she was awarded first place for the innovative idea she incorporated into bedsheets. Just two weeks after this milestone, she received a $25K investment from an enthusiast who believes her idea is clever and has great potential.

Young-Loaeza quit cleaning houses in September 2018 to devote her time to giving life to her inventive ideas. Young-Loaeza was accepted in September 2018 at the University of San Diego in one of their innovation programs, and her company is also a part of a business program at California State University San Marcos. Young-Loaeza has been awarded scholarships to attend the Accelerator Business Program The Brink at The University of San Diego (ranked #1), and The Stella-Labs Women Accelerator Business Program (ranked #5) both listed on the top ten best accelerator programs in San Diego County.

The innovated NEET Sheets, has been featured in several media outlets and has been a part of different programs that believe in its potential. NEET Sheets was also recently awarded a $30K branding project by a branding firm in the San Diego area.

Among other milestones, Young-Loaeza was awarded second place at the annual San Diego Inventors Forum Invention Competition in 2018, in which she was the only female participant among eight competitors.

In the latest months, Young-Loaeza was featured at the United States Patent and Trademark Office website for their 2019 Summer Edition of Inventors Eye Magazine.

She was also invited as a guest speaker at the 2019 Invention-Con Conference that takes place every year at the Headquarters of the United States Patent and Trademark Office in Alexandria, Virginia. Today Young-Loaeza is in negotiations with the well-known company named My Pillow, who after seeing the innovative bedsheets, immediately placed an order.

There are many milestones not mentioned here but we are proud of each one of them. The work has been an awesome and learning experience that is just more enjoyable because the people that have made a tremendous contribution to both Genius On Development and her self. The blessings are beyond what she could imagine simply because of having the habit of wearing faith every day!!

39

THE POWER OF THE "I AM" - DESI ARIAS

The Habit: The power of the "I am"

By Desi Arias - "desideseos-Entrepreneur/Inventor

Why: Saying these negative "I am" statements can not only affect our self-image, but it can also stop any progress on achieving our goals and dreams, as well. We need to stop saying these negative " I am statements" and instead replace them with positive ones. We also need to teach children to say these positive, " I am statements" to themselves. Young people suffer from a wave of self-doubt, self-loathing, and self-destructive statements about themselves. We need to teach them to look in the mirror and find what they love about themselves rather than what they don't like. Saying positive," I am statements" to ourselves is an important habit to create because we believe in and act on what we tell ourselves. If we are constantly telling ourselves the negative, we will produce more of the negative. If we are focusing on what we love about ourselves, we will attract more love, success, money, and happiness in our lives.

I challenge YOU to say, " I am awesome," I am wonderful," "I am loved," "I am a success," and "I love myself just the way I am," every day for 30 days. I promise you will not only feel better about yourself but your life as a whole. It's a choice. Choose to look for the good or the bad in yourself. Your past doesn't dictate your future, so there's no reason you should keep punishing your self for it by "beating" yourself down mentally.

The Un-Habit: Stop telling yourself things that "break" rather than "build" your spirit

Why: You can change your life for the better at any moment. All it takes is for you to point at yourself and say, " I'm not perfect, but I'm okay with that." "I'm striving to be better every day, and I'm starting with saying those positive "I am statements" every day.

As I mentioned previously, when we say we are negative, we believe the negative and the universe matches that which we believe. If you genuinely want to make positive changes in your life, start with the statements you're saying about yourself and others. Negativity breeds more negativity. One little trick to help you change your negative thoughts to positive ones is to practice something one of my psychology professors called "thought stopping." It works like this: If you find yourself saying something negative like, " I'm not smart enough to do that," stop yourself (mid-thought) and look outside or at something beautiful around you. Then replace what you said, with a positive "I am statement" about yourself. Make sure and point at yourself because when you do, you're pointing at your heart. Think of these " I am statements" as "heart statements" because they reflect how you truly feel about yourself.

About Desi: Desi Arias "desideseos" is a teacher-prenuer/inventor. She has been an elementary school teacher for the last twenty-one years. Both in the classroom and out, she uses "I am statements" in her everyday life. She believes there is a lot of power in the "I am statement" because we are defining who we believe we are. Desi lives in San Diego, California, with her husband, two children, two cats, and a dog. She is not only an entrepreneur but an inventor as well.

40

5 - MINUTES OF DAILY GRATITUDE AND SELF-TALK - LOVELY ABBOTT

The Habit: 5 - minutes of daily Gratitude and Self-Talk

By Lovely Abbott - Creative Branding |Social Media
Professional

Why: Gratitude is very simple, yet most of the time, a neglected habit. The little things in life that "good morning' message you got from a family member are just the little things that often take for granted. When you practice gratitude, you acknowledge everything around you and open yourself up for more positive emotions, positive energy. I am a great believer that you attract what you think and what you practice daily. After that, acknowledge yourself. Acknowledge and embrace the greatness in you that whatever that particular day will bring, you are going to rock it!

This little habit, practiced daily will create a collective impact on your daily life by bringing you positivity. This positive energy will encourage you more to take action and do what you do best. It is by choosing how to think and manifest this daily into our lives that you will slowly see the results. For the first few days or weeks, you will feel vibrant and any failure that a particular day may bring won't stress you out anymore. When you start feeling this, you are on the right track. Make a reminder on your phone alarm or calendar. Then try to focus on something positive about your life daily. You will see how it makes a difference with your overall mood and on how you see life as a whole.

The self-talk part if is for you to learn to acknowledge the greatness in you that whatever it is that you put your mind into, you are going to accomplish it. You will find a way to get things done. This little habit, when done daily and religiously, will work wonder. I am sure of this because it did for me. For my first month of practicing this habit, I struggled to push through it because, believe me, when you have been doing things for all your life and then suddenly you break into it, it is not easy. But this habit helped me to get to where I am at today. It helped me to focus more on the positive things around me and the positive things that I can do to the people around me.

Keep going and don't' forget to share this habit with other people to empower them too.

The Un-Habit: Depending your worth based on what society thinks of you

WHY: Societal norms are what stopping women from following their passion. As an immigrant myself, I experienced personally this type of mentality that for the first year in a foreign country, I thought I am not good enough. I felt that I couldn't work on my goals because English is not my first language, and aside from that, I didn't finish a college degree. But if I kept listening to what these norms are telling me, I wouldn't be where I am at right now.

We all should break this habit. Society has its standards, yes, but to stand out and get your goals going, sometimes you have to set your own standards.

I am going to share how I broke this bad habit. The first thing I did was to find a community full of people who are also going through the same thing. Luckily, I found a huge online of Female Immigrants sharing their success and struggles.

I took this community as my home. Their struggles became my inspiration, and my journey started from there.

When you let your weaknesses rule over your strengths, self-doubt will kick in. This will stop you from getting started on whatever it is that you want to do. Remember that the only person on whom you are to going answer for aside from your family is YOURSELF.

Are you going to play the "what if" game? What if you pushed through, what if you did this, and so on...

In this day and age, there are enough followers. What you need to do is to ignore the negativity that society has for you and go for it. Set your own trail because you deserve it.

 **About Lovely:** I am a Filipina mom based in Florida. I am the owner of Lovely Abbot Virtual Solutions. Creative Branding and Social Media are my core services that we offer to entrepreneurs. I run my business from home, all at the same time being a full-time wife and a mom.

As the youngest of 3 girls, I was brought up by my parents to be ready and be as tough as what they say, girls are not only meant to stay in the house. That girls are meant to follow their dreams.

My business is a one-woman show for now, and I cater to at least 5clients during slow months, and in my four years in this industry, I have worked with more than 20 clients already.

I am an Inbound Marketing Certified by Hubspot, a graphic designer, social media specialist, and, most importantly, a woman who wakes up each day with gratitude and dares to work on her goals strategically.

41

LOOK FOR INSPIRATION ALL AROUND YOU - CYNTHIA A. PEEL

The Habit: Look for inspiration all around you

By Cynthia A. Peel - Owner, Peel's Maker Studio, Knowledge Broker, Speaker, Author

Why: Life can become bleak if we fall into a rut and find ourselves uninspired, doing the same thing day after day. We all truly need and crave variety. We also need to feel like we are following our passion and listening to our true inner voices. We need those heart-pounding moments that make goosebumps pop up on our skin. We need the exhilarating whooshing moments that happen when a new idea comes rushing into our heads like darkness fleeing from a room when the light is turned on. It is what I live for. I love that state of awe!

Inspiration can be found everywhere. It sometimes finds me unaware and unprepared. I am sure that is because I have already placed a previous order, that the delivery has just been delayed. I have forgotten about it, like happily finding money in a pocket in your coat from last season. However, typically, I have to go looking for it. That is okay. I enjoy the hunt. Sometimes I will see something while I am driving down the street, or I will hear something on the radio, and it will trigger a whole new line of thought. Very often it will come to me when I am talking with my children, did I mention I have four amazing sons that let me ramble on? Oddly enough, I have found inspiration at the hardware store or the .99 cent store. The cashiers in my small town get a kick out of some of the crazy and inventive projects that I have put together with bits and bobs from their shelves. "What are you going to do with 100 brushes and erasers? They might ask. "Oh, I am making robots for the kids today." Because I have spent the last decade teaching children, I have come to know that inspiration is also easily found just by watching children. They are pure and eager learners, undefiled by social norms that hold so many of us adults back from our creativity. However, most often, I find my inspiration in nature.

Trees surround my favorite place to be. I live near a small community, famous for its Apple Orchards, that borders a National Forest. We have beautiful trees and mountains all around us. I love going outside for a walk or a run whenever I need to think and be inspired. It works every time! I love looking up into the leaves, watching them dance around, and seeing how the light plays on them. I look out over the horizon and the contours of the land. I will sometimes slow down to smell the flowers and watch insects crawl around, or rabbits or squirrels jump out of sight. I appreciate the simple truths of nature. There are so many lessons to be learned by just getting out and observing both flora and fauna. I have shared many of these with my students over the years, and some I've written in my journal, and other more personal lessons stay written on my heart to buoy me up for later.

One of the greatest reasons for seeking inspiration is because it leads to creativity. And creativity will help you solve problems in new and more efficient ways. Our world is quickly changing. We have to be able to adapt and change along with it- to not only survive but to thrive. Being creative and constantly inspired will keep you on your toes, ready for anything that is coming. It will give you the edge that you will need to change your mindset. You will not feel like the world is changing away from you, but that you are adapting right along with it. That you are apart of this amazing new culture and economy that we are creating together. You will have an important say in how our tomorrow is shaped.

This habit has served me well, and I have been able to use it to be creative and adapt and position myself ahead of many changes in a few different industries in my career, including banking and finance, real estate, and education. I'm not saying that I have not had any failures.

That wouldn't be fair. I have. Furthermore, some were painful. I have learned huge lessons from each setback. But the greatest underlying gift that I had, that I can share with you is that I have always been able to rely on my belief that I am here for a great purpose and if I open myself up to inspiration, the next step will become obvious to me. It always works. I know it will work for you too. Look for your inspiration!

The Un-Habit: Giving up

WHY: The worst thing you can do is to give up. You never know just how close you are to your breakthrough moment, and you never will if you give up. I like to picture a story I have heard of the miner underground looking for diamonds. You can see her chipping away at a huge wall of rock. She is exhausted and has no view of just how close she is to her goal, really only inches away from striking through to the mother-load of diamonds on the other side of the rock wall. If she drops her pickaxe in desperation, she will leave defeated, never knowing that she had almost made it. Do not let that be you even if you have to take a break and climb back out to the surface for a while and get some fresh air. That is okay! However, don't you give up! If you want those diamonds, believe they are already yours. See yourself draped in them, sharing them with your friends and family. Figure out how to sharpen your ax and go back down there and hit it! You will breakthrough. Maybe this time, you need to bring a drill instead of an ax or do not go alone, you may need a friend with you, one who has mined diamonds before. You will figure it out. You will be inspired to know how to get your diamonds because they are YOURS! Right?

If you can be refreshed with inspiration, you should see your problem from a new perspective, a new angle that might not have occurred to you before. This great key to problem-solving can open up wonderful and lucrative avenues for you in your business and personal life. It is a technique I had taught to engineering students when we were trying to figure out how to connect point A to B or make a bridge strong enough to hold our robot payload. It is an un-habit that worked when my family was facing a terrible situation during the 2008 real estate meltdown. I refused to give up, against all the odds, when it looked like we could have lost our home. It took much inspiration and creativity, hard work, and sheer tenacity, but we made it through and came out financially better after the struggle. We are only thriving because we did not give up! It does not matter what the problem is that you are trying to solve, coming up with a new and different solution will be vital to your survival in the future economy and your life in general.

About Cynthia: Cynthia Peel, along with her husband, Derek and four sons, makes her home in Yucaipa, CA. She is the owner of Peel's Maker Studio, She is a Knowledge Broker/Author/Speaker.

Mrs. Cynthia Peel is a mom of four talented boys, aged from 11-19. She home-schooled her children starting with

her oldest in 3rd grade. He is now in college and preparing to serve a mission for their church. Cynthia has multiple college degrees and has always had a philosophy to never stop learning. She is a member of the Southern California Robotics Society and a self taught poly-scientist and computer programmer. There isn't a subject that doesn't fascinate her. She gets really excited when she teaches a topic she is passionate about, which are many. She has been known to break out in 'goosebumps' and get all flushed and excited during a lesson. She hopes to inspire that same love of learning in the children she teaches.

One of her degrees is in Economics. She has 20 years experience in banking and financial services and has an entrepreneurial heart. Her business background helps her encourage adults and children alike to imagine how their talents, passions, and inventions could lead them into a new future industry or business of their own, if they choose that path. One superpower Cynthia has is to help other mothers, mompreneurs, to develop business plans that are in line with their passions and talents. She helps them earn income and manage their money wisely so they can support their family's needs while also being there for important moments in their children's lives.

She's had a few other home based businesses, but

focused on Peel's Maker Studio in early 2015 when she was recognized by other moms for the fun way she had been teaching her own boys robotics and various fun science experiments. She has always loved teaching and has volunteered to teach at the local schools and at her church for many years. So it was a natural fit for her to create a business that matched her love for learning and her passion for teaching children. Peel's Maker Studio expanded to hold school assemblies, where they converted the whole auditorium or gymnasium into a discovery science center for the children to explore and be delighted with hands-on activities. The events were covered by the local newspaper and news spread that the Peel's Maker Studio was a fun place for students to learn all things related to S.T.E.A.M. (Science, Technology, Engineering, Art, and Math) They've been growing by word of mouth ever since. Peel's Maker Studio's mission is to inspire their students to be excited learners and problem solvers. They want children to keep their natural thirst for knowledge and to not be bored with their education, but totally inspired by it.

Cynthia also works with parents of home school children to help them inspire their students to be creative and eager learners. It's a big and sometimes overwhelming job being the educator and the parent. But it can be a very joyful and rewarding experience if done right!

Cynthia Peel has served her community in countless hours of volunteer service for over 25 years and has recently been honored by the city of Yucaipa for her efforts to coordinate the Make a Difference Day and

Helping Hands days of Service. She has also been active in the local Faith in Action Committees to help solve the homeless issues. She truly believes that a group of committed and concerned citizens can make a difference and find solutions.

42

PRACTICE TRANSPARENCY IN EVERY ASPECT OF YOUR LIFE - MISTIE LAYNE

The Habit: Practice Transparency in every aspect of your life

By Mistie Layne - Bestselling author, Award-winning Speaker

Why: Have you ever dressed a certain way, acted a certain way, or purchased items you would not typically purchase so that you felt you "fit in?" We all want a sense of belonging because the human race is designed to thrive on community associations. However, "fitting in" presents a problem because often, the ones we try to fit in with are not all they portray to be, and we are left feeling inadequate when we do not measure up to them. Society desires a shift from forming fake and superficial bonds to forming meaningful, authentic, and honest relationships. We need more people living transparently about who they are, what their beliefs are, or what they want in life. I believe with TRANSPARENCY in the open, we become comfortable with who we are as a person, mate, co-worker, and also spiritually. Therefore, we must take accountability for both our success stories in life as well as our failures. When we are honest and open about the things we have done or failed to do, it allows a new level of freedom to emerge within ourselves, which builds confidence and courage.

A habit of being transparent is necessary, so we can learn to love ourselves by realizing we are not alone with our struggles in life. Imagine a world where a young girl feels comfortable talking to her parents about becoming pregnant instead of going to an abortion clinic because she thought that was her only option. With transparency as the norm, the young girl could talk openly with her parents without the fear of judgment, and they could share their knowledge, experiences, and wisdom with her so she can make an educated decision on how to move forward. Imagine a world where somebody having suicidal thoughts could talk openly and honestly with others having similar thoughts. Transparency would show they are not alone and isolated, and having that non-judgemental person to talk to could very well save their life.

Transparency is necessary to educate others so we can JUDGE less and MENTOR more! I founded the #BethatONE Transparency Movement, where I encourage others to step up and share their raw, authentic truth to teach others and prevent the same mistakes. By truthfully sharing our ups and downs with others, we can make the world a better place and ease a little suffering. What adversity have you overcome? Do you have valuable knowledge and insights to share that could benefit others? We all have a story in us, a past we do not want to disclose, or a deep secret we are scared to tell. The truth is that "junk" is robbing us of our future by defining us and weighing us down while we pretend to be something we are not. Start a new habit of being transparent with yourself and others and experience the freedom it will bring.

The Un-Habit: Stop people-pleasing

Why: Are you sick and tired of being sick and tired? Have you fallen into a rut and feel you will never be happy? You are not alone, my friend. One way to start pulling yourself up to a better space is to Unhabit people-pleasing. We must stop depending on others' approval for our validity. Instead, we need our confidence and clarity to achieve full inner peace. With a world of get rich quick schemes, imposters, scams, and people pretending to be somebody or something they are not, we must be careful not to get wrapped up in the dangerous web of trying to please others by "fitting in." It is natural for us to want to please our loved ones, co-workers, bosses, or community leaders, but if we do not have self-fulfillment, we are left stripped of our real identity and cannot possibly experience true inner peace and joy. By discovering what we want for ourselves instead of striving to please others, we reach that feeling of satisfaction. Conversely, if only putting energy and time into trying to please other people, we never obtain satisfaction because the truth is we will never truly please them! We always try and gain others' approval but usually fall short and are left feeling inadequate.

When we stop living our lives for somebody else and truly start discovering what makes us happy, our life will change, and we will have newfound energy and clarity to focus on the things that matter to us. Instead of feeling negative about ourselves, we will begin to notice the positive attributes we have and how we can use them to help ourselves and others. Additionally, when we are solely responsible for our happiness, we can direct the blame where it originates and strive harder to correct our shortcomings. Furthermore, we can also celebrate our successes and give ourselves credit for the wins too.

After escaping and surviving an extremely abusive relationship, I realized I did not even know what kind of food I liked to eat or music I enjoyed because I regularly "gave in" to please my abuser to keep the peace. Furthermore, I discovered my entire life had been about doing what others expected of me or doing what I thought would please them. Growing up in the beauty pageant system in Texas, I learned at a very early age, the power that came with winning and how I could dominate attention by merely doing what others wanted me to do. This behavior is unhealthy and culminates in a loss of self-love, self-determination, and self-awareness.

Fight to find the person you were created to be instead of adhering to expectations of what somebody else thinks you should be. STOP people-pleasing and learn to love yourself. Do not let your happiness be gauged by how other people perceive you.

About Mistie: Are you letting your past rob you of your future by keeping you depressed, ashamed, remorseful, or angry? Mistie went from being a Texas beauty queen at the brink of becoming a surgeon to facing a forty-year prison sentence behind killing someone. Cocaine and domestic abuse robbed her of ten years of her life and led to a horrific rock bottom she courageously describes in her best-selling book, "What Goes Up." Mistie teaches her four-step C.O.P.E.=HOPE method, which implements the release of TOXIC shame and guilt, allowing self-forgiveness and love to lead to true joy and inner peace. After hiding her dark, ugly secrets for years, she now SHOUTS with passion and transparency, how she overcame her worst to live her best. Her message inspires you to face your fears and release the skeletons from your closet. She founded the #bethatONE Transparency Movement, which encourages us to step up and share our raw truth to educate others so we can JUDGE less and MENTOR more. Mistie is excited about globally catapulting her message by recently winning third place in the Next Global Impactor competition. She also founded and hosts "The Flip Side" show and "Raw and Real" deep dive women's retreats. Also, Mistie currently serves as the Vice President on the Executive Board of Directors for Chemo Buddies for Life 501(c)3.

43

CHECK YOURSELF BEFORE YOU WRECK YOURSELF! - SUSANA SOSA

The Habit: Check Yourself Before You Wreck Yourself!

By Susana Sosa - Transformational Coach

Why: As women, our minds are always on two things our to-do list and on other people. We forget to check in with ourselves to see how we are feeling emotionally, physically, and energetically and we also forget to ask ourselves what we want. As a result, we may experience a disconnection to our bodies and operate from a space of being on the go, forcing women to suppress their feelings, which can contribute to why women are now experiencing a higher level of depression, anxiety, and stress. When women make it a conscious habit to check in with themselves, they can experience more peace, focus, and feel more energy to do the things they enjoy doing and can have more clarity in making decisions. Checking in is as simple as practicing these three steps:

1) be aware of how you are feeling at the moment. Observe any sensations or feelings, without any judgment

2) if you are feeling worried, stressed, or down take five deep breaths and change your state of energy by taking a short 2-minute walk

3) notice how you feel after you have taken deep breaths and taken a short walk and notice if your feelings/sensations have changed. The goal is to be at peace with whatever it is that you are feeling. Keep repeating the three steps until you feel a sense of peace. If you are still feeling stressed/worried, be curious about your feelings and ask yourself: I wonder what I can learn from these feelings/sensations?"

Be open to what comes up without judgment and observe from a space of compassion as it can connect you to feelings that you may be suppressing. You can continue to take deep breaths and can make a choice of letting them go. This may not be an easy process and is part of your healing journey. You can also journal what comes up for you and forgive yourself and anyone who may have caused you pain in the past. This can be a powerful experience as not only does it allow you to practice self-awareness and connection with yourself, but it can also support your healing process.

The Un-Habit: From autopilot and passivity to intention and power!

Why: Start your day with intentionality by checking in with yourself in the morning and throughout the day; this will break the habit of going through the day from a robotic, autopilot, and passive state of going from task to task to going through your day with intention, power, and grace. You can start by setting a short intention by creating a statement of how you want to experience your day such as, "I am open to all the blessings I will receive today!" You can then take a few minutes to practice self-awareness and mindfulness by doing a short meditation. Meditation has many benefits and can be utilized for many things, but one of the areas it helps with is to calm the mind to become present to the moment. Do this as part of your daily practice as it will help you start your day in the right mindset, slow things down for you so that you feel more in a flow state, and be more in tune with your feeling/sensations rather than in a fight or flight panic mode. Being in panic mode can have you be in a state of reaction and not allow you to have clarity or connection with your feelings. Being in reactive mode can also block you from making effective decisions, as you may not have the capacity at the moment to think clearly and/or thinking things through. Meditation can also help you feel more peace, focus, have more clarity and energy, and experience more joy in your life. You can also continue to practice meditation throughout your day to continue experiencing the benefits. You can stop you from being in autopilot to being fully in the moment, connected to your feelings, energized to engage in your activities, and having the clarity and capacity to making effective decisions and obtaining powerful results.

About Susana: Susana's mission in life is to support women to step into their power and greatness in a safe and supportive environment with other women to create a life that's full of love, joy, and personal and professional fulfillment. She has a master's in counseling, and she combines her educational background, spiritual training, and intuitive gifts to support women in embracing their feminine energy and experience deep and powerful transformations in their lives!

Supporting other women is important to Susana because there was a point in her life where she was not connected to her power, was unclear about her future, and felt isolated and unsupported. For many years, Susana went from job to job and changing her career focus multiple times because she did not have a clear vision of her career path. This made her feel ashamed and unconfident of her abilities and about her future, since nothing was fulfilling her, and she started to feel that there must be something wrong with her. And although she had many friends her feelings of shame did not allow her to share this with her friends and, as a result, felt lonely, lost, and powerless.

She knew she wanted to support others but when

working with traditional counseling settings and methods she found herself that she wanted to support others in a deeper way. She also realized that she had a special connection to women, as she started to see patterns and relate to the limited beliefs that stops women from accessing their power as well as recognized that like her, women were craving to manifest something deeper in their lives but not clear on what that vision was.

And in her quest to find other methods to help her and women obtain clarity on their vision, transform their barriers, and to manifest that they deeply yearn for, Susana learned powerful practices to help her get connected to the most sacred part of women, her feminine energy. Once she started to embrace her feminine energy, she experienced powerful transformations in several areas of her life which allowed her to get clarity on her vision and life purpose and it also inspired her to step into her power to be visible, self-expressed, and generate the support she needed to fulfill her vision. And now she teaches these practices to other women in safe and support circles so that women continue to heal, grow, transform, shine, and manifest their greatness together with the support of other women.

44

NEVER GIVE UP -EVER! - SHARI MARKS

The Habit: Never Give Up -Ever!

By Shari Marks - Transformational Health Coach

Why: Someone very recently told me how they admire that I always have a positive outlook, how I never give up, & even though I don't always believe it internally, it made me realize that this is something a good habit that I share onto others. Having this mantra or this habit has clearly led me beyond what I ever thought I was capable of in my wildest dreams. I mean moi? Making enough to help us buy a house or buy two new cars or help pay for our kid's weddings?

Funny, I never really gave thought to Habits in the least bit, till the past few years. I mean, I never really examined my action steps, I merely walked through life doing what I do or did.

I decided to become a Health Coach. To my surprise, my health coaching practice grew and grew, slowly but surely. It amazes me since I never thought of it as a business. I was merely helping other people lose weight, get healthy. It has become more of a transformational health coaching program, and now I have a team of health coaches around the country. Go figure? There's been highs and lows, and I've gone through phases yet; I never gave up. I've fired and rehired myself.

My confidence, my ability to keep growing as an entrepreneur, and to grow as a person to become the best version of myself is all based on my not giving up, to keep working on myself to learn the tools I need to become a leader for my coach group.

I just kept helping people. I never dreamed that I was able to buy a house, and cars & pay for our kid's weddings based upon my input to our family finances. This was all because I never gave up trying to find what I was looking for. I have learned to examine and think about the concepts of habits and how they help you succeed in your life.

I once heard that Entrepreneurs are regular people that never give up. You never hear about the people that quit. So many famous people have had many trials and tribulations, were told they would never make it, and yet they persevered and made it!

I never thought I was capable of doing any of the things I have accomplished. Imagine if I had actually planned it out? I attribute my success in never giving up, and keep moving forward, I highly suggest you do the same.

The Un-Habit: Giving up too easily

Why: What if I didn't have the habit of not giving up? I most likely would not have been as independent and would've never bought my own car! I would have still been in a desk job with no real future. If I had given up on my marriage when I was upset about something that happened, I would've given up on many years of marital bliss, which so many people do nowadays. Many couples give up as soon as they get upset about something and don't give it a chance to work it out. I would never have lost fifty pounds and kept it off. I would've settled for second best, in a life of mediocrity which you see so many people do.

Personally, I would never have thought of working on my self-development. I know as my team of health coaches grow, I had to grow and work on myself. Most people would've given up on a group that's not achieving and put the blame on the group or themselves, but I didn't give up and kept pushing myself to grow so I can help them grow out of concepts holding me back or them. I would never have achieved the financial independence that I have. I know I wouldn't have been happy with myself on the inside and would've just lived a life of being a should had.

I can't imagine my life if I didn't have the habit of not giving up and hope you don't either!

About Shari: I lost my Dad when I was merely twelve; life could not get much worse. I must have adapted an outlook of dealing with what I had and making the best of things.

I always felt I was okay at doing things but never felt I was great at any one thing. I don't know that I was ever encouraged to strive for more.

After getting married, I had six kids I had put on a lot of weight from each pregnancy. I tried everything out there, including Bootcamp, for an entire year. I had settled for my lot in life being a big toned up overweight Mommy. At forty-one years old, I felt tired, lethargic. My back hurt, my foot. I finally decided I needed to do something about it. I started many different programs. This time, I wasn't just being a Mommy but finally doing self care. I did not give up, and kept plugging away, but never lost more than twelve pounds on any program.

I came across a couple that had significant weight loss. I was cautiously open-minded. I knew my hubby would probably not approve of my spending more money when I was already paying for the gym and Bootcamp. I ended up doing a program, and l seemingly lost fifty pounds, which was nothing short of miraculous to me. I was smaller than I was at my wedding! Even back to a pre-wedding weight, back to a weight I was in high school, something which most people would never even dream of. I could not believe it! Never giving up, I had accomplished something I never thought possible; therefore, I never even made it a goal or dream.

So many people approached me as I lost fifty pounds. Friends, community members, even a local physician! I figured if I could do this, perhaps, I can help others do so as well. It has empowered me to tackle other areas of my life as well. So, here I am more than ten years later, helping more and more people than I ever dreamed of. I even developed clients and a team of health coaches around the country. I learned self-development and the mantra of being the best version of myself. It has changed my persona and my outlook on life significantly. This has become a lifelong pursuit, which is so inspiring to not only myself but to my group of coaches and clients I work with as well. It is available to anyone who wants to better their life. I strive to look for positive people who want to better their lives as well. I implore you to find what fuels your passion, as life can be amazing until the end.

ACKNOWLEDGMENTS

We greatly appreciate the following contributors for offering their own 1 Habit™s to this book.

• Steven Samblis – Creator of 1 Habit, Celebrity Interviewer, Entrepreneur

• Lynda Sunshine West - Creator of The Women Action Takers Mastermind & Executive Producer of Wish Man the Movie

• Dr. Amy Novotny – Founder the PABR Institute™

• Susan O'Malley MD - Former Emergency Room Doctor, Entrepreneur, Author

• Nichole B. Clark - Author, Speaker & Coach

• Kym Glass - Soft Skills Consultant, Award Winning Speaker and Best Selling Author

• Robyn Jordan - Transformational Mindset and Business Coach and mentor

- Sheree Trask - Writer, Speaker, Rebel, Thought-Leader

- Krystylle Richardson - Leadership & Mindset Expert, International Best Selling Author, Radio Show Host, Red Carpet Interviewer, Missionary

- Sara English - International Coach, Trainer and Speaker with Master Results

- Diana Parra, M.A. - CEO & Founder at Diana Parra International

- Susan D Sharp - Artist, Speaker, Author of Mid-Life Wisdom and 1 Habit.

- Jennifer Harris - Founder & CMO, Brand Builder Rethink Ltd. and BrandInk Agency Ltd.

- Marilen Crump - Creator of the D.R.E.A.M. Success Strategy and Founder of the Female Income Academy

- Cosette A. Leary - Founder of From Welfare to The White House

- Vicky Boladian - Chief Executive Officer of Aerlex Tax Services/Aviation Tax Attorney and Entrepreneur

- Shyla Day - CEO/ TED Speaker/ Activist

- Neelu Gibson - Co-Founder and President, SeaglassRQA LLC.

- Kelly Byrnes - President and CEO of Voyage Consulting Group

- Laura J. Brandao - President of AFR, Inc.

- Jennifer Pruett - Creator of Mind Design

- Mackenzie Watts - Creator of Mindset by Mackenzie/Anxiety Awareness Advocate & Coach

- Lori A. McNeil - International Educator & Business Coach

- Jessica DeMumbrum - Financial Agent

- Ella Glasgow - The Dream Ignitor

- Catherine Turley - CEO of Fit Armadillo®, Bestselling Author, Podcast Host

- Diana Barbiani - Small Business Consultant and Sales Professional

- Katie Mares - Co-Founder, Chief Inspirational Officer Alkamey Group

- Chellie W. Phillips - Author, Speaker and Successfully Ever After Career Coach

- Laura Leist - Speaker, Productivity Specialist and Founder of Eliminate Chaos

- Sara Dudley Campbell - wife, mother of 2, and Realtor at Zeitlin-Sotheby's International Realty in Nashville, TN

- Naomi Bareket - MBA, NLP Trainer, Author, Speaker

- Evangeline Colbert - Victorious Living Coach/Author

- Divya Sieudarsan-Harlall - Author/Youtuber/Fulltime Mama

- Natalie Susi - Teacher, Writer, Entrepreneur

- Irene Zamaro - Founder of Tradeshows Today

- Lea Woodford - CEO of SmartFem Media Group

- Sylvia Chavez - America's Love Queen

- Ruth Young-Loaeza - CEO & Founder Genius On Development

- Desi Arias -" desideseos - Entrepreneur /Inventor

- Lovely Abbott - Creative Branding |Social Media Professional

- Cynthia A. Peel - Owner, Peel's Maker Studio, Knowledge Broker, Speaker, Author

- Mistie Layne - Bestselling author, Award-winning Speaker

- Susana Sosa - Transformational Coach

- Shari Marks - Transformational Health Coach

ABOUT THE CREATOR OF THE 1 HABIT™ MOVEMENT

Steven Samblis created and compiled the 1 Habit™ series by bringing together hundreds of incredible Happy Achievers™.

Steve is the founder and CEO of Envision Media Partners and Envision Media Press. Steve began his business life as a stockbroker, ranking among the top 50 rookie brokers at one of America's largest firms. He has worked with Congress defending shareholder's rights. In 1990, Steve founded "The Reason For My Success," a company that sold self–improvement programs. As the company grew, it expanded into the production of audio and video programs.

Over the years, Steve has traveled North America as the keynote speaker and launched two public companies.

His companies, Envision Media Partners and Envision Media Press, were founded with the mission "To Empower and Inspire people to become Happy Achievers."

The companies do this by focusing on two learning modalities.

1) Book Publishing and Distribution

The company publishes the bestselling "1 Habit" book series. The series is filled with powerful Habits from hundreds of "Happy Achievers™." Habits that have led them to the holy grail of success and happiness.

2) Virtual Reality

The company has developed Envision VR, a Virtual Reality platform for Corporate Training and Personal Development. Envision VR is an advanced alternative to the standard way of delivering inspiring and educational content. It puts the user face-to-face with the world's greatest mentors, trainers, and speakers in an immersive world that provides rapid results.

facebook.com/samblis

instagram.com/samblis

amazon.com/author/samblis

ABOUT THE CO-AUTHOR

 1 Habit About the Co-Author -- Lynda Sunshine West

Live your life with #noregrets has become my life's mantra.

I grew up in a volatile, abusive alcoholic household. Mom and dad were together for 55 years. Dad passed away three years before mom. Two weeks before she passed away, she said, "Lynda, I have so many regrets of things I did not do. Live your life with no regrets."

Those words have stuck with me ever since.

After 36 years working in the corporate world in a variety of positions, the last of which was working for a judge in the Ninth Circuit Court of Appeals, I realized something was missing. I was starting to regret what I was doing, and it did not feel right. I was not happy with my life, and mom's words kept showing up, "Lynda, live your life with no regrets."

So, when I was 51 years old, I embarked on a journey that would take me to places I never imagined.

I hired a life coach who helped me see that there was more to life than what I was living. I realized that if I continued on the path I was on, I would continue to live my life with regrets, so I took a leap of faith and quit my job to become an entrepreneur.

I did not know what I was going to do, how I was going to make money, or whom I was going to help, but I did know what I was not going to do.

I have met some incredible people who have helped me see who I am, what value I have to offer, what I can do to make a more significant impact on the planet, while living with #noregrets. Living with #noregrets means living "on purpose" rather than "on accident."

I have had a lot of ups and downs, have lost and made money, have met amazing people who encourage me, and others who try to beat me down. One thing has always held strong, though: my faith.

I believe we all have a purpose; just some of us do not figure it out until we are a little older. However, it's never too late. Heck, I was 51. I know now that I'm on the right path to make the impact I am here to make.

Along my journey, I created the Women Action Takers Mastermind/Accountability Program to help women gain clarity to attract clients to them, confidence to raise their hand and ask for their worth, and focus on getting faster results. As a result of my work, I have helped women double and triple their income, get off of government aid, create online coaching programs, finish books that have been inside of them for decades, fulfill dreams they have had for many years, and start a new life. This work is gratifying because I am helping them discover their value, share their voice with the world, and live with #noregrets.

I believe we all should live our life with #noregrets because, when we get to our last breath, the last thing on our mind should be, "I had an awesome life and have no regrets."

After all, none of us knows how long we will be here.

ALSO CREATED BY STEVEN SAMBLIS - FROM ENVISION MEDIA PRESS

The book that started a movement.

1 Habit™ Can Change Your Life Forever

You know the joy you feel when you are so passionate about your "why" that you can't wait to wake up and jump right into life? That motivation will get you started, but to be able to follow through, you need the Habits that will help you place one foot in front of the other when things get tough.

Author, Steve Samblis spent years searching the world for the most successful people on the planet. He got to know them and asked them each "What was the one most crucial habit in your life that has made the most significant impact on your success." He then took these 100 Habits and put them into a book called 1 Habit.

Get your copy at http://www.1Habit.com/buy-now